Fan's Eye City

Swansea City in the age of the Premiership

Gareth Phillips

London League Publications Ltd

Fan's Eye City

Swansea City in the age of the Premiership

First published in Great Britain in March 2005 by:
London League Publications Ltd, P.O. Box 10441, London E14 8WR

ISBN: 1-903659-20-5

Cover design by: Stephen McCarthy Graphic Design
                         46, Clarence Road, London N15 5BB

Layout: Peter Lush

Printed & bound by: Biddles Ltd, King's Lynn, Great Britain

Foreword

It is a great privilege for me to be asked to write the foreword of *Fan's Eye City*. Gareth Phillips' book charts the turbulent history of Swansea City through the last dozen years in the context of great changes in the way football is run. These years map an especially poignant journey for me. From the joy of a first win at Wembley to the growing despair, frustration and anger at the way our club was being run and how we as supporters seemed completely powerless to do anything to arrest the slide.

Then came the crisis of the winter of 2001-2002 when the club faced extinction. I can still picture the torment of those long and desperate months. Protest marches, public meetings, rumours galore, the shadowy 'North Bank Alliance', the birth of the Supporters Trust, Mel Nurse, court actions, the defiance of the players under Nick Cusack. But there was also the growing feeling that we - the ordinary supporters - were making a real difference by working together. Out of adversity came strength and events reached a joyful climax when in January 2002, the fans led consortium took control of the club.

Three years later, as I write, the club is profitable, free of debt, making progress on the field and looking forward to a new stadium. We have the opportunity to build a club that is run by fans for the fans and to reach out to a new and wider generation of supporters. I have two young sons who I love dearly. My wish for the future is that they live long and healthy lives and are able to enjoy supporting the new community based Swans.

Leigh Dineen
February 2005

Leigh Dineen is the Swansea City vice-chairman and Supporters Trust representative on the board. He writes here in a personal capacity.

Introduction

One wet evening in April 1968 my late father took my cousin and me to the Vetch Field. In truth, the match itself was less than memorable, although I can still mentally picture the great Ivor Allchurch on the ball, and Keith Todd scoring the winner for the Swans in the dying moments. However, I loved the experience, and have kept on going back for more ever since. They say that first love is the deepest, and although I have since seen much more prestigious matches at more famous stadia around the world, Swansea City have remained 'my' team. From the lows of the re-election era to the ultimate highs of the Toshack years, the story of the Swans has rarely been dull.

However, the last decade or so has been deeply depressing to most fans of the club. Often the off-field story has eclipsed events on the pitch. At a time when British football has gone through massive changes including a huge boom, the Swans have continually struggled. This book is an attempt to make sense of recent history both on and off the field at Swansea City in football's new age. However, the club do not exist in a vacuum, and I have tried to place what was happening at the Vetch in the broader context of events in Welsh, British and European football.

This book doesn't pretend to contain inside stories or salacious gossip. It is merely one fan's view of events at the club. I don't expect everybody to agree with every opinion expressed. Hopefully, however, most readers will empathise with the highs and lows of following the club in the period.

Gareth Phillips
February 2005

Thank you

Thanks are due to Mark Ludlam, Mike Davies, Niall O'Brien, Martin Johnnes, Phil Sumbler, Paul Nicholas, Andrew Thomas, Gary Martin, Colin Jones, Gareth Vincent, Phil Dillon, David Evans and Spencer Feeney for assistance with sources; to Professor David Farmer as the source of much statistical information; to Dai Smith for helping get my writing off the ground, and to Huw Richards for his constant encouragement; to Richard Lillicrap, David Hansel, Dai Little and Jim White for their support and belief in this project; to Mark Bateman for checking the text; to Peter Lush and Dave Farrar at LLP for taking a chance where others hesitated; to Huw Cooze and Leigh Dineen for their assistance at the Trust and Club; to Steve McCarthy for his work on the cover, and to the staff of Biddles Ltd and to Ruth for her support and patience with my obsession and Caitlin for putting up with afternoons at matches.

Finally, to the memory of my late father who took me to my first match at the Vetch, and to my mother for her indulgence in giving me lifts home at unsociable hours after evening matches.

About the author

Gareth Phillips was born in Llanelli. He worked as a solicitor in Morriston for a number of years, and also played in 1980s South Wales bands Andy Pandemonium and Just Bongo. These days he lives in London where he continues to solicit by day and make music by night. He writes the 'Garbo' column for the unofficial Swansea City fans website www.scfc.co.uk, and also contributes to the official club programme.

Chronology

1912	Formation of Swansea Town AFC.
1921	Join expanded Football League in Third Division South
1924-25	Champions of Third Division South – promoted to Second Division
1925-26	FA Cup Semi-Finalists
1946-47	Relegated from Second Division
1948-49	Champions of Third Division South – Promoted to Second Division
1963-64	FA Cup Semi-Finalists
1964-65	Relegated from Second Division
1966-67	Relegated from Third Division
1969-70	Club renamed Swansea City – promoted from Fourth Division
1972-73	Relegated from Third Division
1974-75	Forced to seek re-election to the Football League
1977-78	John Toshack appointed manager – promoted from Fourth Division
1978-79	Promoted from Third Division
1980-81	Promoted from Second Division
1981-82	Sixth place finish in First Division
1982-83	Relegated from First Division
1983-84	Relegated from Second Division. End of the Toshack era.
1985-86	Club are on verge of going out of existence but are rescued by a package put together by Doug Sharpe. Relegated from Third Division.
1987-88	Promoted from Fourth Division via play-offs
1992	Formation of FA Premier League sees Football League divisions re-designated. Third Division becomes Second Division.
1992-93	Reach Second Division play off semi-final but are beaten over two legs by West Bromwich Albion.
1993-94	Win Autoglass Windshields Trophy on first visit to Wembley.
1995-96	Relegated from Third Division after a season of farce.
1996-97	Reach Third Division play-off final at Wembley but lose to Northampton in last minute.
1997-98	Doug Sharpe sells the club to Silver Shield PLC (subsequently renamed Ninth Floor Ltd.)
1998-99	Defeat West Ham in FA Cup and reach Third Division play-off semi-final where they lose to Scunthorpe United over two legs.
1999-2000	Champions of Third Division – promoted to Second Division.
2000-2001	Relegated from Second Division.
2001-2002	Ninth Floor Ltd sell the club for £1 to Mike Lewis who in turn sells on to Tony Petty. Petty's actions enrage fans and possibly threaten the future of the club. Formation of Supporters Trust. Club taken over by local consortium with Trust taking a share.
2002-2003	Survive relegation to Conference with final day win.

Contents

N.B. 'Football' is used to mean association football in this book, rather than as a generic term covering all codes of football.

For the 2004-05 season the third and fourth tiers of English professional football have been re-designated League One and League Two respectively. For the purposes of this book, the divisions are referred to by the names they bore at the particular time. Therefore, for example, the third tier is referred to as the Third Division up until 1992, and as the Second Division for the period 1992-2004 following the inception of the Premier League and then Premiership. Any readers who understandably find this confusing are advised to address complaints to the Football Association and Football League.

Part One: Prologue

1.   Perfidious Albion

The time is around 10 o'clock in the evening on Wednesday 19 May 1993, and I'm travelling south along the motorway from Birmingham. The football season has just ended. More precisely, Swansea City's season will not be extended any further, and there will be no first trip to Wembley.

This has not been a good day, culminating in a disappointing defeat. Being philosophical, however, there had been defeats before and the loss to West Bromwich Albion in the second leg of the play-off semi-final seemed just a temporary set back. Little did we know that the Swans' fifth place finish in the then new 'Second' Division was as good as it was going to get. Or that the club's best team since the heady Toshack era would start to break up almost immediately. That slow decline would set in on the field, culminating in a narrow shave with relegation to the Conference, and that off the field the very existence of the club would be in doubt. It all looked so different back then.

With hindsight, the club's years of apparent retrenchment from 1986 to 1993 could be seen as a sea of tranquillity sandwiched between the frenetic excitement of boom and bust in the period from 1978 to 1985, and the traumas of the last decade. Light had gradually appeared at the end of the tunnel as taciturn Frankie Burrows shrewdly built a team, and even in the depression of defeat at The Hawthorns there still seemed reason to believe that Doug Sharpe's cautious philosophy could take the club slowly but steadily forward. Many supporters felt that the club could build on its best season for some years and re-claim a place at what they felt was a natural level for the club in the new First Division. Sadly, the transfer market activity would come, but as had been the habit during the era of Doug Sharpe's chairmanship, it was not predominantly inward. Rather than strengthening, the club at best consolidated, if not actually weakening the squad. The history of Swansea City from that point onward was to prove a mixture of frustration and under-achievement.

Over the following decade we were never again to finish as high in the league as in 1993. Instead the club gradually regressed, and if there were occasional blips of life, they came in the shape of consolation prizes. Ironically, having failed in one attempt to reach Wembley for the first time via that season's play-offs, the club would appear there twice in the following five years. Other relative highs have included the Third Division championship, and a number of exciting FA Cup runs. Yet the feeling persisted that promotion to and consolidation in the First Division could have been fairly traded for all these crumbs. If not dining at the top table, we should at least have been supping in a better class of company.

Instead, the years since that play-off defeat were characterised by stagnation, broken promises and finally, thwarted opportunism. Fingers can be pointed at the various owners during the period, and accusations made as to the running of the club. Whatever the truth or otherwise of

3

such statements, what cannot be disputed is that these events did not take place in a vacuum, but that football as a whole went through radical changes during this period. Many of the trials and tribulations visited upon the Vetch were to find echoes in other clubs around Britain. Few of us back in the summer of 1993 appreciated the sheer scale of the changes occurring elsewhere that were even then fundamentally changing football.

The Premier League had kicked off the previous August to a great fanfare of media hype which appeared totally disproportionate. What had seemed merely a re-branding exercise of the old First Division was to unleash forces that would change the balance between clubs in a way not seen before. Hitherto unheard of amounts of money would flow into football, and be arguably squandered in an inflationary cycle of player wages and, in some cases, directors' remuneration.

The gap between the Premier League and the remainder of the Football League was to become almost insurmountable, and the idea of the Swans once again gracing the top division of the English Football League was to become increasingly fanciful. For years, clubs had lived on the dream that one day they could put together a team that would sweep all before them. Swansea City had acted out that fantasy once, with an almost fatal return to earth. Over the next decade the chances of such a feat being repeated were quietly moved from being filed under 'unlikely' to a new home under 'nigh impossible'. The Premiership had become what the self styled 'Big Five' wanted all along – an exclusive league of major big city teams with minimal chance of the party being gate-crashed by an uppity little brother. The irony that two of the original 'Big Five' were themselves left behind raised wry smiles, but was of little consolation to those further down the structure.

This book will consider where the brave new world of football has left the Swans a little over a decade on after this revolution began. Logically there seems little reason why a city the size of Swansea should not be able to sustain a professional football club at the same level as the likes of Southampton, Middlesbrough, Ipswich, or Norwich. Yet for years the club has languished in the lower leagues. Most supporters believe that the Swans could be an established Championship outfit, who enjoy the occasional foray into the Premiership. This book considers why we have been unable to achieve even this unspectacular if not unrealistic, vision.

The changes in football over the period have not been restricted to the re-branding and re-financing of English football's upper division. The birth and growth of the Premiership have gone hand in hand with the resurgence in popularity of the game, fired by the media and Sky Television in particular. If the 1990 World Cup saw a change in the way football was presented in the national media, then the early years of the Premiership have witnessed a saturating tidal wave. Football can be seen seven nights a week on television. Fixture lists are changed to accommodate the armchair fan ahead of those attending live matches. In turn, clubs at all levels began to budget on the basis of increasing future television revenues, firing an inflationary cycle that left many clubs in deep financial trouble when the bubble burst.

One area where television has encouraged expansion has been European competition, where Welsh clubs previously had access via the so-called 'back door' of the Welsh Cup. Ironically, in an era when European qualification can be worth vast sums to a club, the Swans have lost their short cut across the English Channel. This book will look at the issue of the Welsh representation in Europe, the whole structure of Welsh football and our part in it.

Beyond events in the world of football, no discussion of football in South Wales can wholly ignore rugby union. While the trials and tribulations of Welsh rugby in the period are beyond the scope of this book, we cannot simply ignore the implications for the Swans, and Welsh football in general, of the seemingly terminal decline of the national rugby scene. Are there lessons to be learnt from what has happened to Welsh rugby, and can football fill the gap? As the fortunes of the Welsh national football team take an upswing, is there a historic opportunity to promote football in Wales, and can the club scene benefit?

As football became perceived as a money-spinning business, with large audiences, media revenue and merchandise market, so appeared corporate man. If Britain in the 1990s became a culture dominated by short term corporate thinking, accompanied by its bedfellow, personal greed, football became a microcosm within that economy highlighting its deepest problems. Old-style local autocrats were replaced by slick new men in suits whose talk was of share prices and stock market quotations, with the jargon of FTSE (*Financial Times* Stock Exchange) rather than footie. Then there was the wealthy super-benefactor who invested huge sums into clubs, turning around their fortunes overnight. Some were genuine and the clubs concerned benefited. Others had ulterior motives. Swansea City was not to fare well in this changing world of high maintenance ownership.

Part and parcel of many a corporate scheme to 'revolutionise' a club was the new stadium. Whilst nobody could deny that the general state of most British football grounds in the late 1980s was appalling, and that change had to come, has that change been at a price which in some instances has been too high? The abolition of standing space, expensive seats, and relative lack of atmosphere all became talking points amongst fans. How did our own plans for a new stadium affect the club, and what will the future hold when such plans come to fruition?

With the new stadiums has come the 'new' fan. Across the country there is an arguable decline in hooliganism at grounds, while ethnic minority and female fans have increased in numbers. Around the same time as we were making our way home from that fateful night at the Hawthorns, the football authorities were taking their first tentative belated steps to combat racism within football. Ironically, this took place at a time when visible racism came to light at the Vetch, while hooliganism always lurked menacingly in the background. What has become of fan culture in its various guises over the period?

On the terraces, or what was left of them, opinion was divided as to the merits or otherwise of football's boom. Some were prepared to take the rebirth at face value, and not ask too many questions as to where the new money came from, or where it went. To those who saw football as yet another leisure activity akin to the latest multiplex cinema blockbuster, such questions probably appeared irrelevant. However, many supporters didn't buy into the idea of football as a branch of the entertainment industry, and began to question the direction the game was taking. If few wished to see a return to the more negative aspects of the game in the seventies and eighties, some did begin to wonder whether football was kissing the wrong suitor.

The growth of fan activism has been a further element in British football over the decade. Many fans tired of seeing their clubs mismanaged, often for the benefit of certain individuals and sought to ensure that supporters have a voice within the game. At Swansea such activism has gone from absolute zero to our current position where the vice chairman of the board is an elected supporters' representative. I will consider the implications and the potential to take the club forward with fans playing an active role.

Driving home that night we had no way of foreseeing the depth of frustration of the decade ahead. At one level an opportunity was wasted which led the club backwards, and in particular led to it missing out on the richer end of one of British football's boom periods. Then again, if we had moved forward in the manner of, say, Huddersfield, would we be in far deeper waters now? With the benefit of glorious 20-20 hindsight, can we recognise and learn from mistakes made by the club in the last decade? Would the club's history have been dramatically altered if certain decisions had been made differently? Would we have been better off, or has our decade of disappointment been a blessing in disguise?

This book looks at the last decade or so of Swansea City, the brushes with success and near-embrace of ultimate failure. From the old style autocratic approach of the Sharpe years, through the grand scale corporate vision of Ninth Floor to incredulous despair as Tony Petty treated a venerable institution with what many regarded as contempt. Out of this at times chaotic history it might be hoped that a model for club ownership can emerge that satisfies the demands of efficient management, but also recognises the club's place in the community.

This book is not a historical narrative of the club in this period, nor does it pretend to have access to inside information or other salacious revelations. Rather, it is based on what was visible from the terraces. It is the voice of one Swansea City fan, but a voice that is not alone as supporters questioned both events at the club and the broader direction of modern football; a return journey through a decade of disappointment that was often frustrating, but which ends with hope of a better future.

2.   How did we get here?

How do Swansea City fans view the club to whom they plead allegiance? Where do we see ourselves in the wider world of football? These may be far reaching questions, but have a bearing on much of what follows.

In recent years it has been almost invariably the case that whenever a struggling lower division club is taken over by new ownership, the incoming chairman will make noises about 'unfulfilled potential' and wildly promise 'the Premiership in five years'. If such claims have some credence in the case of some larger city teams, eyebrows are raised when they are made about the likes of Carlisle United or Darlington. Such populist statements were made when the Swans were taken over by Silver Shield Windscreens in 1997. Could they be taken in any way seriously, or should they have been dismissed as so much hot air?

Certainly most Swansea City fans would deep down consider the club as being 'too big' for the Third if not the Second Divisions, despite that being where the club has languished for nearly 20 years. Indeed, during much of that period clubs such as Crewe and Walsall have enjoyed superior playing records despite being what most Swans followers would consider 'smaller' teams. Why do supporters of the white shirt view their team as underachievers? Is this perception based on more than the traditional inflated optimism and blinkered view of reality typical of the die-hard fan in relation to the team they love? Are Swans' fans just a bunch of hopeless self-deluded dreamers? Would Walter Mitty have found a natural home on the North Bank?

*   *   *

The 50-odd years of the Swans post-war history can be divided into two distinct phases. For the best part of 20 years the club were steadfast, if largely unspectacular members, of the old Second Division. For the best part of 40, the club has drifted along in the lower divisions, with the exception of five surreal years when it enjoyed a whirlwind romance with the upper leagues only to find itself dumped back to where it started. It was an oasis in a desert that proved to be a mirage.

The roots of the idea of the Swans' natural home being the second tier of the English pyramid originated in the inter-war years, and were cemented by the unbroken spell in the old Second Division between 1949 and 1965. Allowing for the Second World War, the Swans spent only two seasons outside the Second Division in 40 years. Many supporters who witnessed at least part of that epoch remain alive today, and have influenced the views of succeeding generations. Certainly, anybody looking at the club in the late 1960s or early 1970s could argue that their presence in the lower divisions was a temporary interlude. The argument, though, grows steadily weaker as the proportion of the club's history spent in the lower divisions increases.

Even behind the myths and legend of the Second Division era lies a tale of spectacular under-achievement. A brief study of the final league tables between 1949 and 1965 shows the team struggling on far too many occasions. Genuine challenges for promotion to the top division appear few and far between. Prior to the Toshack era the main focus of 'what could have been' stories surrounding the Swans focus on the 1955-56 season when the club led the table in the opening months, only to fade following a serious injury to defensive lynchpin Tom Kiley. From there on in it seems the club embarked on a policy of selling its better young players, and fans could only dream of what might have been achieved if a team could have been built around the likes of Cliff Jones, Terry Medwin and the Allchurch brothers. This fantasy didn't even include John Charles who - unlike brother Mel - had been tempted away by Leeds United despite having been on the club's books as a schoolboy.

Therein lies the crux of the frustrations of professional football in Swansea. The area produced a series of top-level footballers. Most achieved success elsewhere. Why couldn't a place that had a reputation as a conveyor belt of talent provide a top class football club that was the pride of the area? While the South Wales industrial belt was in economic decline in the post war period, it was scarcely less affluent than cities such as Newcastle or Sunderland, both of whom enjoyed periods of football prosperity in the era. Those who would dismiss the thought that the Swans could have been a power in British football should consider that the top teams of the day included Preston, Burnley and Blackpool. The maximum wage was still in place, and players' financial demands could not be blamed for either the exodus of talent or the failure to recruit a supporting cast to build success. The main reason for moving clubs surely related to ambition as much as money, and from this distance one can only conclude that the failure of the Swans to enjoy a true heyday lay in the reputation of Swansea as the graveyard of the a-word.

At around the same time as Liverpool and Leeds were stirring themselves out of Second Division mediocrity and becoming clubs that would be forces at national and European level, it seems the board at the Vetch were content to stand still. While Shankly and Revie were supported by their club boards, the Swans developed a reputation as a selling club. Trevor Morris is reviled in the memories of many older supporters as the manager who sold a team, yet surely the blame is more properly laid at the door of those who employed him.

One thing that never changes in football is speculation as to the precise destination of transfer fees, and the suspicion of many supporters was that the transfer policy was not necessarily for the benefit of the club. Whether or not there was substance to this conjecture is impossible to say, for in that era, football clubs were traditionally run as the autocratic hobbies of local businessmen, and financial transparency was never on the agenda. Those were, after all, more deferential times when the ordinary fan was less likely to challenge goings-on in the board room. The concept of supporter input in decision making, hardly universally accepted even today, would have been considered heresy, while the thought of open access to accounts would have made most club owners' blood boil. Discontent was of necessity limited to terrace talk and bar-room mutterings.

Such rumours were to be echoed in the later history of the club, but whatever their truth, history tells us that at that point the club stalled, stagnated and eventually declined. Even allowing for the exaggeration of myths, the records show that during the 1950s there was a bedrock of support for the club in the area. The failure to exploit the club's natural resources was to have the effect of seeing that support and goodwill slowly evaporate to an all-time low in the mid seventies.

By the mid-1960s the most glittering jewels in the club's playing crown had been sold, and the team were spluttering in the league. The cracks were papered over by the epic run to the FA Cup semi-final of 1964, which included the legendary win over Liverpool at Anfield. While there was no doubting the magnitude of the success before the Kop, fewer people asked why the Swans had assumed the mantle of giant killers while Shankly's men wore the clothes of the elite. Just a few seasons before there had been little to separate the status of the teams, as the pre-Shankly Reds spent much of the 1950s in the Second Division, yet now the two clubs were travelling in diametrically opposed directions.

If it might be argued that Liverpool's longer term history was more illustrious, the same could not be said of Southampton, who were also transforming themselves. Instead of lapping up the patronising headlines, it might have proved more worthwhile to ask more searching questions as to why the club were not paying regular visits to Anfield for league fixtures. Instead, the then owners of the club had already embarked on a course that was to subsequently see it visiting Mansfield more regularly than Anfield.

Even then, the thought occurs that the FA Cup run might have been the catalyst for the revival of the club. If luck had been on the club's side, might an appearance in the 1964 Final - in those days the biggest match in the British football calendar - have kick-started a resurgence? Sadly, one suspects not. Even the run to the semi-final should surely have boosted the coffers and lifted levels of ambition. The club had tasted a little of what life at the top table could be like, but showed no appetite to return for a second helping. If Liverpool came to represent Oliver Twist, always hungry for more and unafraid, the Swans were content to remain starving in football's version of the workhouse. The ominous signs suggested a pauper's death was a real possibility. Those in charge seemed either unable or unwilling to read the runes.

This book centres on the apparent decline of the club following a different type of semi-final defeat in the West Midlands. However, the 1964 defeat at Villa Park effectively represented its own watershed in the

9

club's fortunes, which were to run steadily downhill in the ensuing years. If the cup run had resulted in a positive force running through the club, then perhaps Second Division status could have been consolidated. Instead, it seems those who ran the club decided that more of the same was in order. The warning signs of previous years were ignored, the team was not strengthened and relegation followed. Adeptness at accountancy did not necessarily go hand in hand with success on the field. Fairly or otherwise, the fans perception was that the price of so called good book-keeping was relegation.

Defenders of the board at the time might justify their conservative stance by pointing at what happened 20 years later, after the club finally showed the ambition sorely lacking in the past. However, the world of football had radically changed by that stage, and when one considers the manner in which the natural inheritance of the club in terms of locally produced talent and potential support was squandered, one can't help but feel that a historic opportunity had been lost.

What is certain is that disillusion was to spread across the terraces. No club can survive for long on memories, particularly when those memories are of what might have been. Was the golden age in reality no more than a time of wasted opportunity? The undisputable truth was that by the mid 1960s the club was in a poor way. Things were to get worse before they got better.

*   *   *

If the initial 20 or so post-war years had promised much but ultimately proved frustrating, the next 30-odd were to be characterised by great stretches of gloom punctuated by periods of largely unfulfilled promise. Time after time the club appeared to be on the verge of a better and brighter future, only for it to lapse back into mediocrity, brushes with failure, and at times embarrassing high farce.

The club paid for years of underachievement and under-investment by being relegated the season after the FA Cup semi-final. Worse was to follow, as the club struggled in the old Third Division and were demoted once again in 1967. Not even the return of all-time favourite Ivor Allchurch could dispel the sense of decay, and the 17th place finish in the Fourth Division in 1968 was a clear warning that Football League status could be under threat. At that time, before the advent of automatic promotion to and from the Football League, loss of such status was likely to involve reversion to the semi-professional ranks, or even oblivion. The nearby example of Merthyr was a sharp reminder of what could happen, while the ghost of Accrington Stanley haunted many Swans fans and sent shivers down spines. While the next season saw an improvement, there were few signs that a serious revival was on the cards.

Matters were not helped by a young striker called Toshack, who was creating something of a stir at nearby Ninian Park, and the positive impetus in Welsh football lay away from the Vetch. Meanwhile the likes of Gareth Edwards and Barry John were ensuring that Welsh rugby was enjoying a heyday, and many uncommitted sports fans in the area were drawn to St Helens or Stradey Park to witness palpable Welsh heroes in action. The distinctly less than world-class fare on offer at the Vetch was of strictly limited appeal. British football was enjoying the feel-good factor provided by England's World Cup win and the European Cup successes of Celtic and Manchester United. Little of this positive energy was trickling down to the Vetch.

The feeling that the club was underachieving was not, however, limited to the talking shops of terrace and bar. Local lawyer, businessman and fan Malcolm Struel had been a long term critic of the conservative policies of the board, and finally succeeded in putting together a consortium to take over the club. The new regime quickly installed former England international Roy Bentley as manager, and made a limited amount of money available for transfers. Bentley was initially popular and successful as his collection of former internationals and local journeymen won promotion back to the Third Division in 1970 while playing attractive attacking football along the way. The club's title had changed from 'Town' to 'City' and there were high hopes that this change would signal a brighter future.

Having consolidated in the higher division, Bentley's side made a positive start to the 1971-72 season and lay third in the league at Christmas. The Bentley era peaked on Boxing Day 1971 when over 24,000 packed the Vetch for a top of the table clash with Aston Villa. Even allowing for the sizeable away support, this was an impressive gate for a Third Division game, and illustrated the potential of the club. Sadly, the game was lost in the final minute, and the team appeared to lose momentum, drifting down the table in the New Year. Arguably, Bentley's team had been over-reliant on older players, and when Mel Nurse and Len Allchurch retired, various young hopefuls had not proved adequate replacements. A record transfer fee was paid out for former Welsh international winger Ronnie Rees, but he did not make the desired impact, and the money might have been better utilised elsewhere in the team. A disappointing mid-table finish was followed by a poor start to the following season, and the axe fell on Bentley in November 1973.

Bentley was replaced by Harry Gregg, who attempted to shore up the defence, and introduced a more abrasive 'competitive' approach. His innovation of playing wholehearted defender Wyndham Evans as a striker (who said the Dutch invented 'total football'?) certainly surprised and frightened a few opposing goalkeepers, but ultimately failed. At the end of the season the club were relegated. The new board had tried to show ambition, but ultimately Swansea City found itself back at square one. What followed were some of the blackest days the club was to ever see.

The Gregg era continued notwithstanding relegation, and he was allowed to build his own team. Signings such as Danny Bartley and Dave

Bruton served the club well, but others proved disastrous, including Derek Bellotti, a goalkeeper whose antics possessed a black comedic value that raised many a hollow and mirthless laugh from the terraces. Gregg's first full season in charge saw a mid table finish but as the 1974-75 season wore on it became apparent that the indignity of seeking re-election to the Football League was staring the club in the face. With the city situated on one of the westernmost geographical limbs of Britain, the success of such an application could not be taken for granted.

Crowds hit several all-time lows, and the financial crisis grew, culminating in the controversial sale of the Vetch to the local Council. Eventually Gregg resigned with less than half the season left, and was replaced by coach Harry Griffiths, an appointment that was to prove inspired in the longer term, but which at the time was probably partly dictated by economics. In the short term, with no money available to strengthen the team, Harry was unable to turn the ship around, and a re-election application had to be placed in the post. League survival rested in the hands of other club chairmen. Happily, Malcolm Struel lobbied hard and sufficient votes were gained to ensure survival as a professional club.

At this stage supporting the Swans had become a trial of personal strength which might have broken many lesser mortals. Not even being a trainspotter or maker of matchstick models could have been less trendy or exposed you to more ridicule than to admit to supporting the team. Not that many were making such admissions as gates dived below the 1,500 mark. The advantage of such meagre attendances was that you could actually sit on the North Bank throughout the game. The down side, for the most part, was to have to watch it. Many players sported facial hair that would not have been out of place in the popular television show *Planet of the Apes*. Some supporters grumbled that Harry Gregg might have done better to employ the PG Tips chimps. At least we might have got a decent cup of tea at half time.

The consolation was that matters couldn't get much worse, and exciting young forwards Alan Curtis and Robbie James gave some hope that things could improve. Little did we know how. By astutely augmenting the better players of Gregg's team with shrewd bargain signings Harry Griffiths gradually built a side that epitomised attacking football, narrowly missing out on promotion in 1977. With the emergence of Mel Charles's son Jeremy to complete a youthful attacking trio, Griffith's side toyed cruelly with fourth division defences, as a cat with a half dead mouse.

Sadly, Harry wasn't to see his team achieve promotion. Malcolm Struel appeared to sense a moment of destiny, and true to his ambition of augmenting rather than selling local talent, secured the services of John Toshack as player-manager. Harry was to die on the morning of the 1977-78 season's penultimate match with the team on the home straight to promotion. The team were distraught, but won the final two matches to ensure that Harry was given a fitting memorial. Whatever the racier

12

version of the story presented by certain sections of the press, true Swans' fans knew it was Harry's team that won that promotion.

Suddenly, we were supporting a different club. After years of signing other team's anonymous cast-offs, the club was now signing players we had actually heard of. Instead of being the butt of local comedians humour, the Swans were the club that everybody in South West Wales claimed to support. When we drew Tottenham in the League Cup supporters thought of it as a winnable tie, rather than as a good payday with damage limitation as the height of our ambition. Schoolchildren chose to support the Swans ahead of Manchester United or Liverpool. If the political skies over late 1970's Britain were changing and the prospects for South Wales were looking questionable, the Vetch Field represented a little island where all seemed set fair, where the world seemed a paradise of pride and growth.

Players had started to arrive over the summer of 1978, and were to continue to be signed as the season progressed. Instead of bargain-bin purchases to replace a superior departed player, the club was buying to strengthen, and each new arrival signified an attempt to upgrade the team. The Swans grabbed national headlines in September with back-to-back wins over Tottenham at White Hart Lane and Elton John's Watford at Vicarage Road. At the end of Toshack's first full season, promotion to the Second Division was clinched in the final game. In a story that would have been rejected by the editor of *Roy of the Rovers* as being too far fetched, the young player-manager came off the bench to head the crucial winning goal with eight minutes remaining of the season. The city celebrated – the Swans were back where their fans believed they belonged.

It was soon obvious that the 'natural levels' envisaged by most Swans fans and by John Benjamin Toshack were very different things. Suddenly, consolidation was a means to an end rather than an end in itself. Tosh saw the club going to the very top. In an era when Nottingham Forest could be double European Champions and Ipswich Town win the UEFA Cup, who was to say that the name of Swansea City couldn't become respected throughout Europe? Even the most cynical observers were hedging their bets. After a season of acclimatisation, passage to the big time was confirmed at Preston in May 1981. Nobody who was there will ever forget it.

Excitement and expectancy hit feverish levels over the close season. New signings arrived as usual, including all-time club record signing Colin Irwin for £350,000. One suspects that figure may never be bettered. Plans had been unveiled for the re-building of the ground involving the extension of the recently completed East Stand to replace the ageing Centre Stand and Double Decker. When Leeds arrived on the opening day of the season and were sent packing by five goals to one, it seemed nothing could stop the inevitable rise of the Swansea empire. Our time had arrived, or so it seemed. The old elite such as Arsenal and

Manchester United, who surely would soon only be making up the numbers in the queue behind the Swans in the league table, were each given sharp reminders of the new order. Liverpool eventually won the league, but at the end of that first season in the First Division the feeling was abroad that they should be looking over their shoulders. Might the incumbent rulers live to regret allowing the young pretender to leave and set up an alternative regime? That the coup was coming we were certain. It seemed just a matter of when. Tomorrow belonged to Swansea.

Then just as the ruling elite was about to pack the silverware and run, it all went wrong.

*   *   *

Much has been said and written about the roots of failure that second season in the First Division. Possibly we should have sensed that all was not as rosy as it first appeared when the team lost five of the final six matches the previous season. Perhaps the writing was on the wall when the club failed to sign any new players over the close season for the first time in years. Certainly there was ill-luck with injuries that the small squad couldn't afford. The first hammer blow was the loss of defender Colin Irwin to serious injury in September, followed as the season progressed by Alan Curtis and midfield terrier John Mahoney. The loss of the spine of the side that had worked wonders the previous year was crucial, as it became apparent that the club was in no financial position to recruit adequate replacements. At Christmas the situation was far from hopeless, and a good run in the New Year could have still led to a mid-table finish. Sadly, it was around this time that Toshack appeared to lose the plot. Rumours abounded of disputes with senior players and, hamstrung by a transfer embargo, he gradually came to rely on a side full of younger players.

In the end the club failed to beat the drop by seven points, but winning positions were surrendered in crucial matches at relegation rivals Birmingham and Sunderland through conceding late goals. Might these have been averted with a little experience at the back? Goalkeeper Dai Davies may not have been everybody's cup of tea, but surely his experience and organisational skills would have been useful as opposed to throwing the inexperienced Chris Sander into the deep end of what was proving to be a very large pool. Welsh international winger Leighton James departed on a free transfer to fellow strugglers Sunderland, and was to be instrumental in saving them from relegation. Was the need to trim the wage bill quite that pressing? Serious question marks appeared against Toshack's management for the first time, and he appeared to have no ready answers. Were the board too loyal to a man who had brought unprecedented success to the club? Might a change in January or February have altered subsequent history? Could the board have afforded to make a change at that point, even if they had wanted to?

14

If there were those who believed that Toshack should have gone, they were to get their wish the following season – twice over. As the financial woes of the club became apparent and boardroom strife made daily news, pre-season hopes of a swift return to the top flight turned to a fight for survival both on and off the field. One-by-one experienced players were sold at knock-down prices to provide ready cash and cut the wage bill. With around a quarter of the season gone and only one win on the board, Toshack stood down and was replaced by coach Doug Livermore. Little changed on the field and more players moved on. A combination of a depressed transfer market and the realisation by other clubs that Swansea City were holding fire sales led many of the better players to depart for a relative song.

The squad increasingly resembled the youth team, and became cut adrift at the foot of the table. Amazingly, Toshack returned, not only as manager, but also as a player. Whilst his presence managed to conjure a couple of unlikely wins, it was apparent that King Canute had a better chance of turning the tide than the Swans did of avoiding the drop. It was equally apparent that without an injection of experienced players nobody else was likely to have done any better. Partly due to the transfer embargo, nothing changed and Tosh went for a second time in March. Relegation was a formality. Five years after him taking over, and after an incredible ride, the club were back in the lower divisions, where they have stayed ever since.

* * *

When one talks of the era of Doug Sharpe, there are, of course, more accurately two or even three periods. The first followed his assuming control of a floundering ship following the resignation of Malcolm Struel from the chair. Few would blame Sharpe for failing to turn the club around at that point. It was clear that the problems he faced were not solely of his own creation, but the result of previous collective decisions of a board that had arguably got carried away. Upon assuming control, Doug was intent on imposing a sense of financial realism on the club. In the circumstances, few would blame him.

However, the first Sharpe era did not last long and was punctuated by a series of disputes concerning promised investment that led to a period of musical chairs in the boardroom. Eventually, Sharpe resumed the chair some months later. It was obvious that the days of big spending were over, and if the Swans were to rebuild, it would be done by solid and unspectacular means. A wheeler-dealer manager, who could work wonders with limited resources, emulating Harry Griffiths' work of a few years before, was called for.

Colin Appleton arrived from Hull with an impressive record, but must have wished that he had remained on Humberside as his youthful charges continued the depressing form of the previous season. The confidence of many of these younger players must have been progressively shattered as defeat followed defeat. Of all the players touted by Toshack as being the 'future of the club' only Dean Saunders went on to truly achieve, and one can only speculate as to whether the careers of the likes of Colin Pascoe, Darren Gale and Dudley Lewis might have evolved differently given more favourable circumstances.

As it was, Appleton's attempts to bring in experience never bore effective fruit, and by November 1984 the club was again languishing in the relegation places. Crowds sagged as attending games became a purgatorial effort. Rather surprisingly, in view of the financial climate, Doug Sharpe sacked Appleton and appointed John Bond. Moreover, Bond was given some leeway in the transfer market, and managed to sign some experienced old heads. Infamously, he also allowed Dean Saunders to leave on a free transfer, allowing Deano to join John Charles and Giorgio Chinaglia as famous internationals the club allowed to slip through its fingers.

Whatever the long-term effects, Bond's policy did the trick in the short term and staved off relegation. However, this was a reprieve rather than salvation, and the club struggled again the following season. By this stage, though, form on the pitch had become of secondary importance as the financial storm clouds that had been gathering finally unleashed their might. Survival as a club became paramount, and relegation was seen as almost a reasonable bargain if it meant seeing the club live to fight another day. Friday 20 December 1985 was a bleak, cold, wet, winters day. Yet the gloom in the sky was as nothing compared to the gloom in hearts as Swans' fans read the early editions of the *Evening Post*. All the worst fears of the preceding two years had been realised. The Swans had been wound up. Next day's game against Walsall was off. Seventy three years of sporting history were now set to become as much part of local history as the Mumbles Railway.

Thankfully the club never went the way of the old red trams that once inhabited the same part of town. The next few weeks saw frenetic activity as various factions organised in an attempt to save the club. With a prescience that was to find echoes 26 years later, local business adviser Roger Warren Evans suggested involving a fans' co-operative. At that time few took this as a serious proposition, as there was little precedent in British professional football for such an institution and little mechanism to turn such idealism into reality. Fan action was focused in the Swans Aid campaign which raised a rumoured £60,000 to assist in the rescue effort, but for which fans received little save for a pat on the back. Supporters' representatives on the board were not part of the agenda in 1986.

In the event, the successful package that allowed the club to continue was put together by none other than Doug Sharpe, beating off a rival consortium consisting of Mel Nurse, Harry Hyde, Dave Savage and Peter Howard. At the time, few cared as long as the club survived. The ins and outs of the period in which Doug Sharpe assumed control in his own right form the next part of the story, and are the subject of wildly differing views amongst the team's support. Whatever was to happen in the future, the fans and the city continued to have a club to support. For that, if nothing else, Doug Sharpe wrote himself an important place in the history of Swansea City.

*   *   *

Whatever the whys and wherefores of the Toshack years, they have had a profound effect on the collective consciousness of the club ever since. With hindsight, it is easy to say that the years of success on the pitch were matched by incompetence off it, and that we lived recklessly beyond our means. Yet there were few dissenting voices at the time. Malcolm Struel was merely putting into effect what every Swans supporter had been urging for years. We didn't sell our best young players, we speculated to accumulate. Sometimes the margins between success and failure can be very narrow. If we had enjoyed better luck with injuries and had managed to hang on in the First Division, might history have turned out differently?

Certainly Struel believed that the West Wales public never backed the club sufficiently. These claims have been leapt upon by sections of the Welsh media, and have become almost an article of faith amongst those who believe that the only football club in Wales worthy of top division football is Cardiff City. However, to many regular fans, the claims of there never having been any sell-outs at the ground in the era will cause a quizzical twitching of eyebrows. Those who remember terraces without an inch to spare in games against Leeds and Manchester United would question where the missing fans were supposed to fit. While tales of clubs deliberately under-declaring gates may amount to little more than bar room gossip, most fans of the time have an anecdote surrounding the dubious practices of turnstile operators.

However, it is certainly true that many of the secondary fixtures in 1981-82, against the likes of Stoke City and Notts County did not attract big gates. Moreover, support in the second season was hugely disappointing. Therein, perhaps is a clue to the real problem. The club had enjoyed six seasons of continual success when gates had risen six-fold. On any analysis this was a massive level of growth. However, it also probably meant that for too many of these 'supporters' loyalty to the club was little more than skin deep. When the novelty of seeing the top teams had worn off, and particularly once the tide of results had turned, too much of this 'support' proved fickle.

Perhaps if the club had fulfilled its potential in the 1950s or stayed in the Second Division in the 1960s and 1970s, the bedrock of support would have been there. As it was, years of failure and resultant disillusion had seen too many people drift away. In building from an average gate of around 3,000 in 1976-77 had the club come too far too soon? Perhaps if the Toshack era had commenced in the Second Division with core support of around 10,000, history would have evolved differently.

Yet the psychological consequences of the era were to live with the club for years to come, and bring us back to the question posed in the opening section of this chapter. In terms of self-perception, are we a big club that has fallen on hard times, or a small club that enjoyed a Warholian period of fame? This is a question with no simple answer.

Objectively, history tells us that the club spent 40 years in the old Second Division, save for a short spell largely attributable to Adolf Hitler, followed by the best part of the last 40 in the lower divisions, save for a similarly short interlude attributable to John Toshack. To see us as a large club in such circumstances is delusion. Yet we have enjoyed times and produced a supply of players that eclipse the likes of Hartlepool and Torquay. In terms of potential, a city the size of Swansea should be quite capable of supporting a club within the top two divisions, but the reality of recent performance speaks for itself. Despite the ornithological nickname, the club in some senses is neither fish nor fowl.

More subjectively, the years in the top division appear to have had an effect on many supporters' psyche. There seems to be a little part of all of us who witnessed the events that does not truly accept that the club fell as quickly as it had risen. In the same way as the tales of the 1950s were passed on to a younger generation, so the legend of the Toshack years has become imbedded in the souls of all who support the club. Are Swans fans collectively in denial as to the true status of the club?

In the early 1990s the club was about to be asked where it stood, as football's class divide widened. The limitless indecision that had characterised so much of the Swans' history was about to see them be caught out of time. More than ever, the schism between supporter perception and prosaic reality was to grow wider.

Part Two: The Sharpe end

3.   Faraway, so close

Swansea City kicked off the 1992-93 season with a 1-0 defeat beneath the bleak moors of North-West England in the depressed former textile town of Burnley. Two teams whose football fortunes had declined with the old industrial heartlands, yet both still believed that they could one day relive former glories. A few hundred miles to the south, a fixture took place involving another Lancastrian team that viewed with hindsight, encapsulates the journey that football has travelled over recent years.

The newly formed Premier League kicked off that August amidst a frenzy of media hype, particularly in the press owned by Rupert Murdoch, hardly surprising in the light of the Premier League's potential effect on the fortunes of the Australian media tycoon's Sky Television. The new league had ostensibly been born out of the FA's desire to provide a new domestic structure to help the England team and generally improve standards. The fact they would also give their administrative rivals at the Football League a political bloody nose was an added bonus. The FA's avowed ambitions coincided with the desire of England's major clubs to obtain a larger share of television revenues. Throw in a satellite television station desperate for a major ratings coup, and the league that was to shape British football in the new millennium was born. Whether its influence has improved football at anything beyond a superficial level is a difficult question. Looking back to that summer of 1992 we appear to be looking at a very different world.

The opening fixtures pitted Chelsea against Oldham Athletic: a game that featured one of the traditional big names of English football against a club who had assembled a fine team under manager Joe Royle, and who were enjoying a rare spell in the top division. The subsequent history of the two clubs tells us much about how the inception of the Premier League has changed the face of British football.

Fast-forward by just over a decade to the summer of 2003, and it became difficult to remember that, this was an opening fixture Chelsea fans hoped, rather than confidently believed, they could win. During the close season of 2003 Chelsea spent in the region of £50 million on an array of international stars, while Oldham were on the verge of financial oblivion and struggling to retain the journeymen who had helped them to the previous season's Second Division play-offs.

However, beneath the immediate surface differences between the way the two clubs had developed lay an even more complex tale. Chelsea themselves had been facing financial meltdown as a result of decisions taken in the era of the 'new' football and had only been rescued through the sale to a Russian multi-millionaire. The prospect of a similar figure rescuing Oldham seemed unlikely. For all their financial problems, Chelsea had become big international business, and now lived in a world that made them ripe for such a take-over. Oldham, like many traditional

21

smaller British clubs were hanging on to life by a thread.

Yet that afternoon the impact of the new league set up appeared limited to the new green shirts sported by the officials, the absence of a full fixture list due to television re-scheduling and media hype disproportionate to what was essentially the same old product.

One look at Stamford Bridge in 2003 says a great deal of the changes at Chelsea. Today the ground features a sparkling new hotel and leisure complex centred around a state of the art all-seat football stadium. Yet in 1992 it was a combination of spectacularly failed 1970s ambition and crumbling concrete terrace bowl. The difference between Stamford Bridge and the vast majority of British football grounds could be measured in terms of sheer size rather than quality. There were more seats at Chelsea than at Oldham or Swansea, and the terraces were larger, but the actual facilities were largely indistinguishable. This was reflected in admission prices, which were only marginally higher in the top division.

The differences between the upper classes of the English divisions and their less illustrious smaller brethren were of degree rather than substance. Chelsea, as a big city club who had spent most of their history in the First Division enjoyed a larger general level of support than the likes of Burnley, Oldham or Swansea, and, as members of the top division, a larger share of the old television deal money. Yet the difference was not so large as to place them in a wholly different world in terms of potential player recruitment.

In August 2003 virtually any player on Chelsea's substitutes bench would have walked into the 1992 starting line-up without second thought, although the nearest the likes of Juan Sebastian Veron would have come to the London club in those days would have been flying over the club's Heathrow training ground en-route to some more appealing cosmopolitan venue. In the new millennium Chelsea, Veron wasn't even necessarily considered for a place on the bench, as the cosmopolitan squad was rotated with one eye on the opulence of the Champions League

In contrast, both sides played largely British born teams for that opening Premier League fixture. The only foreigners in contention were Norwegian defenders Erland Johnsen of Chelsea and Gunnar Halle of Oldham. Chelsea may have proudly fielded their record £2m signing Robert Fleck, but there was a sense that they had truly pushed the boat out, and the majority of their team were homespun youngsters such as Graham Le Saux, Graham Stuart and Eddie Newton. Oldham were a typical combination of home developed talent and bigger clubs' cast offs such as Andy Ritchie. They might not have had the financial muscle to land Fleck, but it would have not stretched credibility for them to have competed for Chelsea's other debutant that day, much travelled striker Mick Harford. Oldham were to later sign former Swan Sean MacCarthy from Bradford. Football's family tree had not then grown so that the branches were unrecognisable from one another.

Having said that, despite the romantic purism of fielding home-grown players, the reality was that much British football was not actually very good. Since the mid-1980s there had been a preponderance of teams playing percentage long-ball football and this permeated all levels of the game, including the Premier League. Howard Wilkinson's workmanlike Leeds had just pipped Manchester United to become the last champions of the Football League in its traditional format. League domination was but a pipedream for Alex Ferguson at that time. Arsenal's brand of powerful direct football kept them in domestic trophies, but their Champions Cup ambitions had been put in stark context when Benfica embarrassed them with slick passing at Highbury. England had just returned from an equally humbling exit from the 1992 European Championships in Sweden, where Graham Taylor's inadequate tactical nous at international level had been exposed.

In the lower divisions there were a high percentage of teams playing direct football, although some such as the Swans kept the flame of the skilled passing game alive. Ironically, there was not the gulf in playing standards between the top and lower divisions that was to develop. Squads were smaller and because wage differentials were not as great, players were spread more evenly around the leagues.

Oldham were typical of a phenomena that had regularly shaken English football's more complacent self styled big guns. While Chelsea, Newcastle and Manchester City had in the recent past fallen from grace, albeit temporarily, cheeky upstarts such as Brighton, Notts County, Watford, Wimbledon and, yes, Swansea had stolen their moments in the limelight. While only the 'Dons lasted any length of time in the top division, the adventures of the others provided a counterpoint to the predictable noises made by more usual suspects for domestic footballing honours. Even allowing for Liverpool's pre-eminence in the final years of the old First Division, serious challenges had come from such diverse sources as Ipswich, Norwich, Nottingham Forest and, yes, Swansea. Today, a serious Premiership challenge from outside three or four 'big' clubs might prompt the traditionally lethargic Football Association to send the dope testers out.

The Premier League, combined with the new look television coverage, new grounds, influx of skilful foreign players and the Bosman ruling were to change the face of football in Britain. What we had yet to anticipate in 1992 was the sheer scale of those changes, and how they would break football's family apart.

The sums of money generated in the top league exceeded all expectations, and many individuals involved both on and off the field boast incredible personal fortunes, while elsewhere clubs totter on the edge of financial oblivion. The dream pursued by Swansea, Watford and Wimbledon now appears open only to those who have become the playthings of the rich, while some clubs pay a huge price for pursuing the dream that makes the Swans' near fatal debts of the mid-1980s appear small change.

There was little doubt that football had to change. Afternoons spent dodging between potentially lethal animal pens and neo-war zones while watching brutalised football were likely only to appeal to an ever-decreasing audience. There was certainly a need to revolutionise the product on the pitch and to fund the better facilities off it. However, many would question whether the path football has taken toward these destinations is the right one. Has treating football as a branch of the entertainment business, with its moral welfare to be entrusted to entrepreneurs, created a distortion of sporting and community ideals?

Has football changed irredeemably? Is it wholly inconceivable that one day, given good management and a little good fortune, a future generation of Swansea City footballers can emulate the likes of Curtis, James and Charles and compete with the best in Britain and Europe? At the time of writing such a prospect seems even a greater pipedream than it did in either 1975, or for that matter in 1992. Back then, it still seemed possible that Swansea City could again line up for a league fixture at Stamford Bridge in the not too distant future. In 1992-3 we were, after all, still playing essentially the same game.

*   *   *

In truth, few Swansea City fans were overly optimistic on the eve of the 1992-3 season. There had been little in recent seasons to suggest that the team were moving forward with any true sense of purpose. The preceding three seasons had each seen a poor start, mid-season revival and late season slump leaving the club hovering too close for comfort over the relegation places. The best that many supporters hoped for was a season of mid-table mediocrity, while the more pessimistic could see a long hard struggle to avoid relegation. The club had to all intents and purposes reverted to its 1950s character, seemingly content to drift along while selling its better players.

When Doug Sharpe had originally put forward his package to save the club, few had dissented from the chairman's expressed desire that the club should balance the books. During the first few years of the second Sharpe era, fans stoically accepted that survival of the club was paramount. 'No return to boom and bust' might have been emblazoned as a motto beneath the revived club's badge. Relegation from the old Third Division was accepted as a reasonable price of survival, and following the revival in fortunes during Terry Yorath's first spell as manager, the sales of Terry Phelan and Colin Pascoe were grudgingly accepted as the new reality. Many fans could see that both players were moving to clubs in the higher divisions, and serious discontent was prevented by promotion back to the Third Division via the play-offs in 1988.

However, frustrations grew during the first season back in the Third Division as the good start made by Yorath's team dissipated due to a lack of goals, and finally disappeared with the manager's departure to

Bradford City. The lack of scoring potency was particularly galling as Sean MacCarthy had been sold to Plymouth for a modest £50,000 on the season's eve. MacCarthy was not everybody's hero, but he did subsequently prove himself to be a consistent journeyman goalscorer, while his former team were reduced to using defender Andy Melville as a makeshift striker. The growing feeling that the sale was a false economy was fuelled when £35,000 was paid out for Hereford striker Stewart Phillips who was to prove, putting it politely, too little too late.

There was also suspicion on the terraces that, despite Terry Yorath's publicly expressed reasons for moving north, the relative ambition of the two clubs may have not been altogether absent from his decision. In his subsequent autobiography Yorath stated what many Swans' fans had thought at the time, that domestic reasons were not his sole motivation. As far as the fans were concerned, losing good players to First Division Wimbledon or reviving Sunderland was one thing. When traditional rivals such as Plymouth and Bradford were viewed as more attractive, some serious questions were prompted.

Subsequent seasons yielded only frustration and mediocrity, both under Ian Evans, and following Yorath's chastened and prodigal return. Frank Burrows' initial season in charge had done little to excite the city, while better players such as Chris Coleman and Andy Melville left the club. In fairness, Doug Sharpe did allow some money to be spent, notably in the 1990 close season when Jimmy Gilligan and Terry Connor were signed to form an anticipated potent attack. Sadly, this partnership never fulfilled its potential, although Gilligan would surely have been more effective but for injury.

In the supporters' eyes too many good players had been allowed to leave, some to clubs that Swans fans had great difficulty in stomaching as being 'bigger', while too frequently money had been spent on inferior replacements. Few sensible fans expected the reckless spending of the Toshack era, but there was a feeling that Swansea City were going nowhere.

The summer of 1992 had seen yet another departure as Coventry paid £250,000 for John Williams. While the transaction represented a good profit on a striker that some supporters suspected possessed little more than naked pace, and allowed the player a genuine opportunity for betterment, it fitted a pattern that suggested the club were not serious about moving forward. Too many people in the area had simply given up on the club, and this was reflected in a gate of around only 3,000 people for the opening home fixture.

Expectations were so conservative that few fans had been particularly depressed by the opening day reverse at Burnley, and indeed, compared to previous recent opening day debacles at Stockport and Leyton Orient, this was no big deal. Slowly fans had come to expect little, and generally this was what the club delivered. It was therefore something of a revelation when Mansfield were beaten 4-0 in the first game at the Vetch.

Without ever suggesting that they were about to walk away with the league, the team built on this encouraging performance, and a 2-1 victory over ambitious Reading at the Vetch in October saw the North Bank break into a chant of 'We are top of the league'. Younger fans probably had to be taught the words and tune. Sadly, this was to be a short-lived addition to the North Bank repertoire. A 4-2 defeat at Orient the following week was the last time this particular paean to success was to be used for some years. Still, the team were looking in good shape, and for the first time since Yorath left for Bradford there was a genuine hope that the club could challenge for promotion.

Looking back, the squad was arguably the strongest at the Vetch since the Toshack team of a decade or so earlier. Roger Freestone had returned to Wales from Chelsea, and for the first time since Michael Hughes was forced to retire there was a feeling that we had a genuine match-winning goalkeeper. Keith Walker and Mark Harris had forged a strong defensive partnership behind a midfield of Russell Coughlin and John Cornforth. The latter was an astute signing, arguably Burrows' best, providing the side with a genuine playmaker, while the veteran Coughlin bustled with energy and neat passes.

The spine of the team was completed by one of two contrasting close season signings in a lone forward role. Both players contributed vital goals during the course of the season. Both were to also display cardinal personal traits at the season's climax, to mixed effect. Colin West radiated class and control and gave ample evidence of the qualities that had persuaded Glasgow Rangers to sign him. He was also to show an attitude that had possibly led to them unloading him. Meanwhile, competition for his place came from Andy MacFarlane, a muscular beanpole signed from Portsmouth.

The enigmatic MacFarlane was certainly wholehearted, and could produce moments of skill and score important goals. However, he could also be rather ungainly and few Swans fans could confidently predict what might happen next when the ball went in his direction. In the event of a player missing a simple chance, television pundits are fond of using the rather euphemistic phrase 'He'll be disappointed with that'. It was difficult to tell whether MacFarlane was disappointed with some of his efforts, as it was often impossible to know what he had intended in the first place.

However, the side's most promising individuals, all of whom were to leave under Doug Sharpe's sell to survive policy, were in the wide positions. Des Lyttle was the archetypal Burrows signing, using the Swans as a staging post on his journey from Dr Martens League to Premiership. In the opposite full-back berth, Steve Jenkins confounded the opinion of Terry Yorath who had previously considered releasing him, and was to go on to win a number of Welsh caps.

Over the course of the season the floppy-haired Jason Bowen was to develop into the rising star of the team. Playing a role that alternated between wide on the right and support striker, Bowen's pace and skill were to prove devastating against Second Division defences. Playing a similar role on the opposite wing was Andy Legg, finally putting paid to the theories of those who said his presence in the team was solely down to his record breaking long throw. Legg was to score a number of impressive and vital goals, none more spectacular than a volley against Stoke that would surely have been a contender for 'goal of the season' had it been scored in the Premier League.

However, a key component in the bright start had been Colin Pascoe, back at the club on loan from Sunderland. Pascoe represented the last link with the Toshack era, having been blooded at the age of sixteen in the old First Division. Sadly, his youthful promise had been diluted as the team plummeted down the leagues and the skill that saw him score a superb goal against Aston Villa in 1983 more often than not attracted unwanted attention from guileless defenders at a loss to stop him by fair means. Two broken legs were the result, and we only saw flashes of what might have been a very special talent. A transfer to Sunderland had seen him play at the top level once again, but he had seemed unable to fulfil his potential. Coming home to the Vetch had seemed a good move for both parties, and in his role just behind West he had supplied genuine creativity. However, Pascoe returned to Roker Park in November and the rot set into the Swans' season.

Large sections of the support believed that once again ambition was being thwarted, and pointed the finger in Doug Sharpe's direction. Fairly or otherwise, many fans believed that the team was being undermined not so much by a failure to break the bank as a failure to break the piggy bank. Following a disappointing home defeat by Brighton that confirmed the team's drift into mid table, it all became too much for some supporters who protested against the chairman.

Terry Connor returned on loan from Bristol City to no great effect, and there was almost a feeling of reliving the past at the Vetch as players from different past eras came and went. More permanent relief of the void filled by Pascoe's departure was provided when former Arsenal and Celtic attacker Martin Hayes arrived in the New Year. Hayes is not remembered fondly by some sections of the Swansea crowd, and whether he was ever fully fit is a debateable point. However, when he was on form Hayes provided a breath of genuine class in the team, and some of his perceptive running and passing were outstanding. He also weighed in with a number of well-executed goals, although the one best remembered by most Swans fans was a two-yard tap-in against Cardiff City at Ninian Park in a televised 2-1 Autoglass Trophy win. The fact that Hayes could not conceivably have missed barring a thunderbolt from on high was simply neither here nor there. Sometimes, context is everything.

By the New Year the team were in mid-table, yet as a result of postponements held home games in hand on most of the teams above them. The original dates for many of those games had seen the team in indifferent form. The re-scheduling was to prove invaluable, as the team galloped through the closing stages of the season, winning five out of six home fixtures. However, the team had been beaten 2-0 at Reading in the final away fixture, depressing not only for the result, but also for the delays caused by trouble erupting amongst a faction of Swansea supporters. Crucially, Jason Bowen was stretchered off in the win over relegated Wigan that clinched a spot in the play-offs.

The Swans were to meet West Bromwich Albion in the play-off semi final, which was a mixed blessing. Albion manager Ossie Ardiles typically employed a skilful attacking approach that arguably suited the Swans better than the more physical confrontation promised by the other play-off contenders, Stockport and Port Vale. On the other hand the Baggies had run out 3-0 aggregate winners in the two encounters in the league season proper, and with the second leg at the Hawthorns would almost certainly attract a large and vociferous support.

If West Wales and heavy rain are synonymous in the minds of many, they were not let down as 16 May 1993 dawned. The rain poured, the mist swirled and the crowd bayed as the Vetch took on the appearance of some sort of Celtic hell for the men from the Black Country. Older supporters might have been reminded of the Villa Park semi-final of 1964. Again a freak goal was to cost the Swans dear.

After a scoring drought in a flood-affected first half, the game swung dramatically toward the Swans early in the second. The ball was crossed into the Albion box and there was Andy MacFarlane, skidding across the water like Twizzle on a surf-board to extend a gangly leg to unfeasible heights and drive the ball into the net. Joy turned to ecstasy as Martin Hayes provided a class finish to double the lead and surely put the club firmly en route to Wembley. However, we had forgotten that nothing is ever straightforward with Swansea City.

With the game in its closing phases an Albion set piece was repelled but the ball was played back in and flicked high over Roger Freestone. Andy MacFarlane rushed back to cover his goal line. In one of those split seconds that seems to take an age, the ball hung in the air and glanced off the bar before bouncing off MacFarlane's leg into his own net to give the unfortunate striker a second, less welcome, entry on the score-sheet. With hindsight this can be seen as a cruel stroke of luck on a player conscientiously helping out in defence for the sake of the team. Yet in the immediate aftermath of the match there was a feeling of frustration that Albion had been allowed back into the tie in the most exasperating way.

Still, the result meant the club went into the second leg with a lead, and the more optimistic supporters saw an omen in the 1988 play-off final against Torquay, when the scoring had followed an almost identical pattern. The theory went that if the team could see off Albion's initial onslaught and quieten the crowd, the tie could still be won.

Within the opening quarter of the second leg, all best laid plans had gone further west than any part of Bromwich. Two early goals for the Baggies meant that the Swans were behind on aggregate almost before some people had taken their places. Needless to say that silencing the crowd had been struck off the early agenda. The Albion fans pogo-ing up and down while shouting 'Boing, boing' was one of the more amusing and impressive sights around British football grounds. Suffice to say that few Swans fans appreciated it at that moment.

Yet by the second half the team had dug in, weathered the storm and were slowly but surely creating chances. Just one goal could take the tie to extra time. Albion's Mellon was sent off for a violent two footed lunge, and suddenly the balance of the tie could be felt to be shifting ever so slightly back toward the Swans. One goal against ten men was all that was needed. Sensing the moment, Burrows threw on Colin West as an extra striker. He certainly changed the game, but not in the way that either Burrows or the increasingly noisy Jack Army wanted.

Within minutes of taking the field West stuck out a spiteful stamping foot and the referee delivered the inevitable red card. As to what was in West's head at the time one can only speculate. In practical terms it meant the advantage swung back to the blue and white stripes, and left the final outcome stark. No goal. No Wembley. No promotion.

Yet some would argue that an opportunity had been lost earlier in the season when Colin Pascoe departed back to Sunderland as his loan expired. The team suffered their worst run of the season in the aftermath, and while there was a recovery in the New Year, some supporters believed that had the club made Pascoe's return permanent at that stage that a genuine challenge could have been sustained for an automatic promotion spot. Whilst fans of all teams are wont to idle speculation over what might have been if things had been handled differently, with Swansea City this was becoming a recurring theme.

*   *   *

If the 1992-93 season had been largely positive on the field, there were depressing aspects off it. The crowd trouble at Reading was not the first instance of Swansea men behaving badly, but was then the most serious and high profile incident. Sadly, as we shall see, it was not to be the last, with direct and indirect financial consequences to the club. However, equally depressing for most Swansea fans and probably not entirely unconnected was the appearance at games of a group who openly identified themselves with racist causes and politics of the far right.

The broader reasons behind such political and social phenomena are complex and a detailed analysis of the causes is well beyond the scope of this book. Suffice to say that post industrial South Wales is a place where disillusion and alienation are widespread, and there is little doubt that such conditions represent fertile breeding ground for extreme views. Whilst in one sense this is a social problem that is broader than the football club, where such activities directly affect Swansea City then the implications should not be ignored.

The rightwing 'British' movement had raised its head in various aspects of youth culture in Britain in the late 1970s and 1980s, both in rock music through the following of cult bands such as Sham 69, and also on the terraces of certain football clubs. For years the football authorities looked the other way and pretended that there was no problem of racism in British football. Ironically in season 1992-93 they finally stopped pretending that the problem could be swept under the carpet forever, and gave official backing to the "Kick it Out" campaign.

Up until the early 1990s there had been little indication that this was a phenomenon that particularly affected Swansea City. Undeniably, there had been instances of individual black players being targeted for abuse, and it would be naïve to deny some of the off-hand racism that took place on the terraces and stands at the Vetch. However, this was low-key stuff of the type that occurred at many sporting events in Britain then, and while often unpleasant and unacceptable, there was little sense of such behaviour being systematic or orchestrated.

However, this particular season saw the emblematic flying of the Union Flag at Swansea matches, a move which if nothing else, certainly seemed to surprise the fans of opponents. While at one level, there can be argued to be nothing wrong with flying the British flag, context is all, and the subtext on this occasion suggested a rather different message to Geri Halliwell's mini-skirted take on 'Cool Britannia' a few years later.

To say that politics has no place in football altogether is naïve, and recalls the disingenuous declarations of rugby union administrators of the 1970s and 1980s when they claimed that the two should never mix. Certain football clubs have overt political connections. Celtic and Rangers are an obvious example in Scotland. The respective status of Real Madrid and Barcelona in the context of Spain following General Franco's victory in the Spanish Civil War is also well known, while Athletic Bilbao have unambiguously adopted the mantle of Basque nationalism. In East Germany, Dynamo Berlin were the team of the hated Stasi (secret police) and by extension the hard line communist regime.

However, football in England and Wales has been largely free of such overt associations, and it's difficult to think of a team in either country that one would immediately and seriously associate with particular political causes. While Tottenham, for example, are often associated with the Jewish community, this is not a qualification for supporting the club.

In particular at Swansea there has been no overt connection between the club and any particular cause, and the club has always been taken to be representative of the area and little else. For the majority, the Vetch was somewhere that politics could be set aside, and the people get behind their team, irrespective of individual party sympathies. You might not necessarily agree with the man next to you on the North Bank, but as long as you both spent 90 minutes supporting the team, such differences could be set aside. However, far from setting political views to one side, this particular group sought to impose them on others.

The vast majority of people who support Swansea City find the views of this group offensive and their displays annoying and unpleasant. Most people who attend matches at the Vetch have no truck with extreme racist or sectarian attitudes. This was perfectly illustrated during a match with Colchester United in August 2000 when the visitors' young black striker Lua-Lua was racially abused by a certain section of the crowd. The putative Newcastle and Portsmouth player went onto score a superb goal in the second half, probably one of the best pieces of individual skill seen at the ground that season. The overwhelming majority on the North Bank broke into spontaneous and sustained applause. Lua-Lua responded by applauding the crowd. Both knew a point had been made.

Indeed, the traditions of the Swansea area are a long way from the style of politics that were being espoused by this small group. After all, Swansea was one of the centres of the industrial revolution, when people poured into the area from England, Ireland and even parts of continental Europe as well as rural West Wales. Most current residents of the old industrial belt around Swansea were descended from these economic migrants. If the origins of these immigrants seem parochial in today's globalised world, their arrival did create a cultural melting pot of its day. This huge influx of workers was to be at the heart of the radical non-conformism that was typical of South Wales from the late eighteenth century onward. South Wales became synonymous with the Chartists and Rebecca rioters and was a cradle of the labour and trade union movements. Unlike South East Wales, the Welsh language remained strong in Swansea's hinterland, and suburbs such as Morriston possessed a strongly Welsh identity. It was in this vibrant cultural melange that organised spectator sport was born and where Swansea City had its roots.

The Swans have seen involvement, on and off the field, by a broad range of social and ethnic groups. On the field, its greatest FA Cup giant-killing featured an epic performance by a goalkeeper from the Irish Republic. The club's only ever goal at Wembley was scored by a black Englishman. Its most successful team was pieced together by a Jewish lawyer, and the descendant of Scottish immigrants. If it is to have a future in a world where spectator sport is a marketable commodity then it must emphasise that multi-cultural tradition and reach out actively and inclusively to all parts of the local community

That those who openly espouse extreme causes are an unrepresentative minority is evidenced by the fact that they tend to come out of the woodwork for fixtures where there is a likelihood of trouble. Few such people are to be seen supporting the team on a wet October Wednesday in Scunthorpe. Fixtures against the likes of Millwall, Hull, Plymouth and, inevitably, Cardiff tend to be the catalyst for their attendance, making for a thoroughly depressing and unpleasant experience for the majority of well-behaved die-hard fans who havc to put up with over-the-top policing and a poisonous atmosphere. Few but the most committed of decent supporters would want to return for more.

The potential adverse effects for the club ranged from straightforward financial penalties for misbehaviour by fans to a more subtle frightening away of support. Realistically, most people don't want to attend matches where there is an above average danger of being inadvertently caught up in crowd trouble, or of an unpleasant atmosphere as a result of racist or other inappropriate chanting.

If the club wished to draw on a wider base of support then it seemed action was needed to deal with the twin threats posed by crowd violence and racism. Not to do so risked frightening away potential support. Sadly, successive administrations failed to effectively attack and eradicate these problems that were to resurface and plague the club throughout the period covered by this book.

4. Adventures in Metroland

Consolation for football teams who have underachieved in the league is traditionally found in one of the many cup competitions that are strewn liberally across the British football season. A top ten finish and a run in one of the cups is often used to excuse the type of season that never really got off the ground as far as a championship or promotion bid is concerned. So it was for Swansea City who didn't quite manage to the top 10 place, but did indeed have a cup to cheer. Maybe it was not the sort of big, ostentatious, flashy cup that got covered on *Match of the Day*, but a cup all the same.

For the first time in years most Swans fans were feeling genuinely optimistic about the forthcoming season. The previous season's play-off place suggested that promotion to the First Division was not just a pie-in-the-sky dream, but a real possibility. In the aftermath of defeat by WBA many felt that if we could effectively replace the disgraced Colin West that a promotion spot was not beyond us.

Slowly, however, as the summer wore on a more familiar uneasy feeling spread through the support. Few were surprised at West's release, but more quizzical eyebrows met the departure of Russell Coughlin to Exeter. Whilst hardly in the first flush of youth, Coughlin had formed an effective central midfield pairing with John Cornforth and to permanently dismantle the previous seasons' midfield platform struck many as premature. Had this been the full extent of the departures then few supporters would have relapsed into worry. As it was, at least one of the two other losses left many once again questioning the clubs ambition.

Nottingham Forest signed Des Lyttle for a fee of £375,000 which certainly represented a huge profit on a player who had only arrived from the Dr Marten's League a year earlier. Most realistic fans appreciated that Lyttle was being offered a higher grade of football by the former European Champions in his native East Midlands. However, more disappointing was the other departure to the same city when Andy Legg left for Notts County for £275,000.

Legg had just enjoyed his best season in the white shirt. Had he signed for a major club most fans would probably have been philosophical. However, Notts County had been a team whose fortunes the Swans had regularly traced over recent years, and despite being a division higher and having recently refurbished Meadow Lane, most Swans fans found it difficult to think of them as a bigger club. That Legg saw Notts County as a more attractive proposition seemed a sad indictment of the Swans present condition.

In fairness, Doug Sharpe did make funds available for the transfer market, even if the sums added up to a higher income than expenditure, particularly after the club received a windfall from the sell-on of Andy Melville. Notably, £125,000 was paid to Exeter for full back Andy Cooke, while £20,000 was paid to the same club for John Hodge. Cooke was to suffer bad luck with injuries while tricky winger Hodge came to represent good value for the fee. More questionable was the £110,000 spent on Steve Torpey who never truly cut the mustard as West's replacement, either as prolific goalscorer or effective target man. Mark Clode represented Burrow's traditional bargain, arriving on a free transfer from Plymouth. However, the real excitement was caused by Colin Pascoe's £120,000 return from Sunderland. Many felt that the previous year's promotion push fell away when Pascoe returned from loan to Wearside, and that he might complete a useful attacking midfield. Strangely, the skilful Pascoe was to be employed in a more withdrawn role than in his previous spells at the club, and some questioned whether his apparent use as Coughlin's replacement was truly playing to his strengths.

Despite the disruption to the team, the early results promised a good season as three out of the first four games were won. Sadly, this was about as good as it got in the league. As summer waned the club started to fall like the autumn leaves. Two good performances in the League Cup against Premiership Oldham encouraged the optimists, but the club's mid-table league position was a major disappointment. As autumn turned to winter, the skies were not the only gloomy thing in Swansea. Consistent only in their inconsistency, the season to date was encapsulated by a 4-4 home draw with Blackpool where a two goal lead was thrown away late in the game, while Andy MacFarlane clumsily missed glorious chances to clinch the game. Matters reached a new low in November with a defeat in the FA Cup at Nuneaton. Anybody suggesting that this was to be a season of cup glory would have risked being diagnosed as having a serious mental health problem.

However, if we thought that matters couldn't get any worse then we were to know differently before Christmas. The ugly scenes of violence witnessed at Ninian Park plumbed new lows even for a fixture that had become notoriously fractious off the pitch. The 1-0 defeat left not only the Swans facing the prospect of a relegation battle in the second half of the season, but many fans questioning whether they really wanted to be there to witness it. Question marks were later raised about the Police tactics on the evening, and in particular the indiscriminate placing of all Swans fans in the grandstand. Supporters who had no interest in becoming involved in trouble had reason to rue the decision to generically bracket the Swansea crowd together. Innocent fans had to brave the hail of missiles as much as those who were enthusiastically joining in.

A section of the crowd on each side viewed the match as an occasion to cause mayhem, and the resultant scenes that appeared on local television news programmes did little to convince the wavering potential supporter that football in Wales was worth going out and supporting. Doug Sharpe certainly decided that enough was enough. Henceforth there were to be no away fans at the fixture until further notice. The sad truth was that the derby clash had become associated in the minds of the broader public with unacceptable levels of violence. Few but the die-hard fans of either club, or committed troublemakers, would want to endure the prison camp conditions that attending the fixture involved. In the end, it seems the clubs opted for damage limitation and, in the circumstances, few impartial observers could criticise them for that.

Despite the Swans' increasingly worrying league position, the team hadn't actually been playing badly, but as in that Blackpool game, missed chances and sloppy defending were contributing to a season of underachievement. A run of six games without a win had precipitated the pre-Christmas slump. However, a win at Bristol Rovers in the final game of the year kick-started a sequence of eight league games without defeat that lifted the side back into mid-table, where they remained for the rest of the season.

Moreover, the improved form coincided with the appearance in the fixture schedule of a number of games in the Autoglass Trophy, a competition derided by many, but that was to save the team's season. Much of the improvement could be attributed to the loan signing of Matthew Rush from West Ham, who provided a skilful dynamism in midfield. Rush seemed to provide the midfield spark that had been missing since Russell Coughlin left. Cruelly for both the player and the Swans, West Ham recalled Rush during March, meaning that he missed out on the Wembley final. Burrows acted quickly, signing Dave Penney to plug the gap, having also signed Kwame Ampadu to strengthen that part of the team in February.

Many fans were wondering, however, whether the loss of Colin West was being equally felt. Love him or loathe him, there was little denying that on his day West could be a class act and without him the side lacked a target man to truly lead the line. Further, it was obvious that the team were not scoring enough goals, and while we may not have previously seen the best of Jimmy Gilligan due to injury, there was no doubt that without him the team lacked a player with the potential to score 20 goals in a season. This was something that was to plague the club for a number of years, and during the 1993-94 season neither Torpey nor MacFarlane looked likely to solve the problem.

Certainly Torpey was proving something of a disappointment, taking until November before registering a league goal, while his general play lacked both the assertiveness of the true target man and the positional sense and desire of a natural goalscorer. Instead, the main threat came from Jason Bowen who was developing into a quick and dangerous player in his withdrawn wide role, and who contributed a total of 14 goals. He was also attracting the attention of the likes of Newcastle, and Swans fans were already steeling themselves for one of Doug Sharpe's 'balance the books' speeches.

The salvation of the season started in unlikely circumstances before Christmas, with a rather circuitous ride around the West Country. Plymouth and Exeter were beaten in the ill-attended group stage, before the vagaries of the Autoglass rules led to the Swans meeting Exeter once again in the first round of the knock out stage. There was something of a feeling of *déjà vu* about the tie in the light of the previous season's FA Cup saga when we had been forced to play a further game against the Grecians having ostensibly knocked them out of a cup. Still, the match did provide the comedy highlight of the season, as the Swans' clinching goal came care of a farcical error by the Exeter goalkeeper who contrived to totally miss his kick when dealing with a routine back-pass. Comedian Freddie Starr was associating himself with the West Country team at the time, but probably realised that he was unlikely to ever come up with anything quite as side-splitting. Certainly there was more giggling than fervour on the terraces that night, for the competition was still not enticing the Swansea public through the gates.

Public perception was turned on its head when the Swans won 2-0 at Orient in the next round, one of the best performances of the season. Suddenly the team were in the so-called Southern Final, with the genuine possibility of a visit to Wembley. Again, the team belied its erratic league form to beat Wycombe 3-1 in the home leg, and by holding the strangely nicknamed 'Chairboys' to a single goal defeat at Adams Park, the historic trip that had escaped the club in 1964 was sealed.

Nobody could pretend that the Autoglass Trophy was commensurate with the FA Cup. However, consolation prize or not, after so many years of being not so much the bridesmaid as the devout nun who watches from the outside while others are showered in confetti, the Swans finally had an invite to a big day in one of the world cathedrals of football. The truth was, of course, that deep down most of us suspected that a cup run such as that of 1964 would never be repeated. We were therefore not likely to get all sniffy and look a gift cup final in the mouth.

Okay, we were not going to get the chance to sing *Abide With Me*, or any of the other stirring wartime ditties encouraged by the strange man in a white suit on top of what looked like a set of airplane stairs, but we were to see our team emerge from the famous tunnel and take the seemingly endless walk to the half way line. For anybody who annually throughout childhood had spent the first Saturday of May glued to the televised jamboree that was the FA Cup Final, this was no small thing. In those days we were led to believe that the whole of the world was watching the pictures from the Empire Stadium. To some Swans fans, it seemed that it was enough that this particular game was being shown live in Cardiff.

Cynics called it a Mickey Mouse competition, but as anybody who has been to Disneyland will tell you, Mickey Mouse is big business. To put it in context, nearly 49,000 people turned out for the match. Throw in that most of the fans of Swansea and Huddersfield had travelled over 200 miles to the game and one realises that this was a genuine event. One can't help but think that only the truly miserable would denigrate a day out that thousands enjoyed in the world famous old stadium.

Almost inevitably, the game itself was something of an anti-climax. Andy MacFarlane gave the Swans an early lead but Neil Warnock's typically robust Huddersfield side powered their way back into the game to equalise. Ideally, we would have won the match in open play, and were a whisker away as Jason Bowen's fine run ended in a shot that came back off the post. In the end we settled for a win on penalties as John Cornforth, Kwame Ampadu and Steve Torpey all kept their heads better than their Huddersfield counterparts. If nothing else, the shoot-out did give Roger Freestone the chance to save a penalty before the twin towers, even if he probably wouldn't regard it as his most difficult save.

Then we cheered and sang and watched the team lift the cup, celebrated at our end and drank far too much in London in the evening. After all, it wasn't everyday that you got to see the Swans win at Wembley. The top 10 finish would have to wait – but for now we had lifted one of the cups!

*   *   *

If there was one disappointing aspect of the club having made its Wembley debut in 1994 as opposed to 30 years earlier, it was the state of the self-styled venue of legends. In 1964 the stadium had been recently refurbished in anticipation of the forthcoming World Cup, and at the time was probably amongst the finest in the world. By 1994 Wembley looked considerably better viewed from a distance. Seen from the Metropolitan Line the Twin Towers looked down imperiously from their hill, both a ghost of the architectural splendours of the late colonial era, and a reminder of the supposed technological white heat of 1960s Britain. Up close the ground was more symbolic of a late millennium decline. Standing rather forlornly in the midst of the grey industrial estate that now occupies the site of the Wembley Exhibition, it seemed to epitomise a shabby Britain that attempted to make over the cracks. The Empire may have become a plc, but few could pretend this was modernity.

To many Swans supporters the stadium would have been disappointing, but possessed a familiar feel. After all, the Vetch itself was a ground that was part of local legend, but had gradually become run-down and in need of massive refurbishment or replacement. The toilet facilities and limited catering outlets at Wembley would have seemed home from home, although not even the Vetch presented sight-lines as appalling as the first half-dozen rows at Wembley. When hype and emotion were set to aside, Swans fans who had visited the redeveloped Cardiff Arms Park would have thought Wembley distinctly second-rate.

Ironically, that same Arms Park, considered by some the finest sports stadium in early 1990s Britain, was to be deemed outmoded before the decade was out. The state of the art Millennium Stadium rose on the banks of the Taff, a pronouncement of pride and identity by Wales to the world. In contrast, both Wembley and a home for the Swans became the centre of grand designs, thwarted plans and lack of action.

Reports surrounding various schemes for relocating the Swans had been circulating since the 1970s. The limitations of the Vetch Field site were viewed as inconsistent with the clubs ambitions even at that stage, and the subsequent hardening of the Taylor recommendations into law put matters into even sharper relief. If the club were to have a future in the top two divisions of the English League pyramid, they would have to play in a ground that contained a viable number of seats. This was no longer an option, but a legal requirement. The only question was whether to develop the Vetch or to move on.

The Vetch, like many traditional football grounds, was crammed into available space between the terraced houses and other furniture of urban life in an industrial town. Some would say it was appropriate for some sections of the support that it was sited en route between a brewery and a prison. The densely packed football terrace was as part and parcel of industrial Britain as steelworks and steam engines. Now the steelworks are pruned, the steam engines in museums and terraces only a memory in the upper echelons of football. Society had changed and football had to move with it.

Yet there was a huge emotional tie for the club at its traditional home. This was, after all, the ground where the majority of Swans fans would have seen their first professional match. Memories remain of epic matches played over the best part of a century, and the word 'Vetch' had become synonymous with football in South West Wales. Many of the all-time greats, not only of the club, but of the world game had appeared on the old cabbage patch. The names of John Charles, George Best, Bobby Charlton, Kevin Keegan, Ossie Ardiles, Kenny Dalgliesh and George Weah could be added to a list of club men including Ivor Allchurch, Cliff Jones, Robbie James and Alan Curtis. The small pitch, shoe-horned between the gardens of neighbouring houses had been the scene of epic drama, fantastic skill, memorable glory and broken dreams. If the club moved, a little part of us as supporters would die. Our hearts cried out to remain at the Vetch; our heads began to doubt that it was practically possible.

Perhaps the last great opportunity to develop the Vetch had gone with the crash of the 1980s. The new East Stand that rose proudly on the site of the awkward hunch-backed, railway sleepered terrace was the concrete embodiment of the Toshack dream. The terrace it replaced was a fine place to bask in the sunshine, but not for the faint hearted in a typical West Wales squall. This was to be the first phase in a wholesale redevelopment of the ground. Malcolm's Struel's vision would have seen the new stand extend around three sides of the ground, replacing the Centre and West Stands. In the event, the cost of construction became part of the financial albatross that nearly cost the club its existence.

By the late 1980s the cracks at the Vetch were starting to show. First the new safety requirements following the Bradford fire in May 1985 led to closure of the top tier of the Double Decker – few fans ever called it the West Stand - robbing the ground of one of its best vantage points. Then a safety check prior to the start of the 1988-89 season condemned the rear of the North Bank, severely limiting capacity. A ground that had once held 32,000 people had become restricted to around half that number. Perhaps a defining moment came when the top tier of the Double Decker was removed in 1991, as the resultant gap changed the character of the ground irretrievably. A useful screen against the sun on brighter days, and a cosy shield against the cold winds that swept in from the direction of Mumbles Head, the ground always seemed a little less atmospheric without it. For many years the great green monster with 'Vale of Neath Ales' emblazoned on the front had been the defining backdrop to events on the pitch, and like an amputated limb, many of us could still sense its presence long after it had gone.

One catalyst for Struel's grand design was the lack of seating accommodation at the ground, which cost the club revenue during the glory days. The Taylor report upped the ante beyond economics and a serious debate ensued in the early 1990s as to the future home of the club. A move to a redeveloped Morfa stadium was mooted, but nothing materialised. Certainly Doug Sharpe seemed unable to convince the Council of the worth of his plans. With little movement on the Morfa project, the possibilities of redevelopment of the Vetch were once again explored.

The prime difficulty with the Vetch was that the compact location and strange angles that contributed to its unique character also made the building of new stands difficult. The Struel regime had already learned an expensive lesson in the law courts as the residents of William Street won compensation for the detriment to their environment caused by the East Stand. To implement the original plan would have almost inevitably involved further compensation payments, if not the need to purchase and demolish additional properties. By the early 1990s the cost of even gaining sufficient space for new stands seemed beyond the club, let alone actually building them.

Attention turned to building a new stand on the North Bank side of the ground. Whether the pitch should be moved, allowing for redevelopment of the Centre Stand was a moot point amongst supporters. The terrible risk of such schemes is that if finance runs out, the team is left with what might be called 'Molineux syndrome'. This was a condition suffered by Wolves in the 1980s whereby both touchlines were huge distances from the crowd, and stands that at one time gave a fine view directly behind the goal suddenly become adjacent to the corner flag. In the end such discussions became academic as planning consent was never obtained. In reality the Vetch was living on borrowed time, although some of us imagined in our minds eye what might have been if Malcolm Struel's original vision had been combined with a new North Bank Stand. Supporting the Swans has always involved much thinking along the lines of 'if only' and this was another to add to a long list.

Arguably, however, the single most significant development surrounding the ground in the era of Malcolm Struel's chairmanship was not the building of any stand, real or projected, but the sale of the freehold to the Council. Controversial at the time, some supporters doubted the wisdom of the transaction in 1975, although in reality there was probably little alternative. However desperate the original motives, with hindsight the move was a masterstroke. One can only shudder at the thought of what might have happened had the freehold of the site fallen into the wrong hands. The fate of both Brighton and Wimbledon illustrates quite clearly the danger of a club losing control of its home. Whatever other accusations can be levelled at the Council, their presence as the club's landlord has probably saved both the ground from unscrupulous developers, and by extension, the club its existence.

Yet if the Council had effectively ensured that the Vetch continued to be a football ground, they also stood accused of prolonging the club's stay at the ground through failing to allow plans to build a new stadium to come to fruition. The issue of a future home for the Swans was to develop into a saga that was to last throughout most of the period covered by this book. Neither Doug Shape nor future owners Ninth Floor were able to deliver the new stadium.

By the mid-1990s, as other clubs opened impressive new stands or moved to shiny new stadia, the Swans remained at a Vetch Field that was looking distinctly tired and out of time. Much loved as the Vetch may have been, its condition was becoming symbolic of a club that was in a run down state, and that seemed to have been left in a time warp as the wider world of football moved on.

*   *   *

If Swans fans felt a sense of frustration and despair at the club's form in November 1993, then they were to suffer twice over that month as the Welsh national team's campaign to reach the USA World Cup finals came off the rails in inimitable last match fashion. Even given Wales's previous track record this was an excruciating near miss as Paul Bodin's penalty crashed back off the woodwork to dampen and finally extinguish Welsh hopes. Added to the despair of the 1978 and 1986 qualification campaigns, it became all too obvious that penalties, World Cups and Wales didn't mix well.

Failure to qualify resulted in a huge loss of opportunity to raise the profile of football in Wales, which historically had played poor relation to rugby union in terms of perceptions of national identity. Certainly the timing would have been opportune, for few would have argued that contemporary Welsh rugby was a good vintage. With economic change cutting deep in South Wales, the nation needed a boost to morale, while the appearance of the football team in the World Cup Finals would undoubtedly have lifted the game's profile.

Domestically, it was likely that interest and participation in the game would have increased, with a potential knock on effect on club attendances. Certainly the fortunes of the game in England were turned around in part by the success of the national team in the 1990 World Cup, and while there is possibly some truth in the argument that Welsh participation at USA 1994 would merely have heightened interest in the more high profile Welsh stars in the Premier League, there must surely have been some spin off for the local club scene.

Sadly, for Wales it was not to be in 1994. In the aftermath of this near miss, post mortems centred on Bodin's penalty, Mark Hughes suspension and Terry Yorath's tactics. Yet while there may have been something in each of these arguments, what they failed to address was a more basic truth. Wales had come a poor second to their visitors in terms of technique. While it was true that Wales had a handful of players who were as good as any in Europe, in other respects it seemed that the Welsh team were far off the technical norms of the international game. It was ultimately self-deluding to blame the failure to reach USA 94 on a penalty miss. Obvious failings needed to be seriously addressed; the opposition simply passed the ball better, kept possession when necessary and generally showed greater technique, tactical acumen and imagination.

Wales had as many stars at the time as many international teams; the difficulty was that the journeymen who made up the remainder of the team looked second best in terms of technique as compared to their opponents. One can never create genius, and the truly great will always be accidents of birth rather than creations of a system. However, what the system can do is firstly ensure that the truly gifted are developed in the right way, and possibly more importantly, ensure that the more average talents are developed in a way that turns ordinary players into technically competent ones.

Why is it that Wales seems unable to produce sufficient numbers of players of technical ability and tactical acumen to compete at international level? While there will always be the excuse that we are a small country, this does not explain why other small countries are able to attain such goals. If size is everything then how have Holland become one of the most feared nations in world football? Does the real, and more uncomfortable, explanation lie in the manner in which young players were being developed? Was Britain, and in particular Wales, out of step with the rest of the world? Moreover, was there any correlation between the answer to this question and the apparent drying up of the flow of top class players that came through the ranks at Swansea City? While it is true that the latter issue is slightly more complex, and will be discussed in greater depth elsewhere in this book, the overall question must be asked as to whether as a nation and as a club we are necessarily developing young players in the correct way.

As the decade progressed, the question became more pronounced, partly due to the Wales team descending into a period of gloom and despondency, and partly due to the British football public becoming more accustomed to seeing the superior technical standards of the foreign imports into the domestic leagues. Whether Swansea City would be able to help supply the answer was an interesting question.

5.   The dragon has two tongues

One European connection for Swansea City was about to come to an end as the 1994-95 season approached. This was to be the last season when the Welsh clubs that played within the English pyramid system were allowed to qualify for the European Cup Winners Cup via the Welsh Cup. The very nature of one of Wales's few genuinely historic sporting competitions was also to change while, at a time when European competition was becoming increasingly high profile, Swansea City's chances of participation were becoming remote, and for the foreseeable future had come to an end.

The move ostensibly had its roots in the Welsh FA's desire to protect its own independence, and that of the national team, in the light of increasing pressure from other members of FIFA to bring the anomalous situation of the four 'home' countries participating in international competition into line. Certainly, there had always been rumblings from outside Europe as to what was perceived as a hangover from colonial times. The FAW sought to assert its own identity by setting up its own national league system, and to base eligibility for the Welsh Cup and its associated European entry on membership of the new pyramid.

Many people suspected that the FAW had a rather more radical agenda up their sleeves and saw the move was the thin end of a wedge designed to force the Welsh clubs playing in the English pyramid into the Welsh set-up. The history of the formation of the League of Wales was thus to become one of the most divisive issues ever to occur in Welsh football. While much of the story is outside the parameters of this book, the broader arguments inevitably raised question marks as to what the future held for Swansea City.

The most obvious problem was that Wales had been extremely late in attempting to set up a 'national' league. In attempting to do so around a century after the other home nations, the FAW would inevitably be superimposing their vision onto an existing reality that had established traditions. That there had been no previous national league structure for Welsh club football lay in the way that the game had developed in Wales in the late nineteenth and early twentieth centuries.

The economic imperatives of the industrial revolution dictated that transport links were built laterally toward England rather than longitudinally to improve the traditionally poor communications across the hills and mountains that divided north and south Wales. The northern coal and steel belt around Deeside fell within the orbit of the industrial powerhouses of Lancashire, and football soon spread west across the border. Meanwhile the mines and metalworks of the south had been largely financed from Bristol, and the shakers and movers of the developing communities had brought rugby with them across the Severn. Consequently, football faced an initial fight to become established in the area in the face of virulent establishment opposition.

Indeed the chief sponsors of professional football in South Wales were not the FAW who were based in far away Wrexham, but the English Southern League who were engaged in a turf war with the Football League, and saw the area as potentially fertile missionary territory. Whilst the Glamorgan League did re-invent itself as the Welsh League and harboured ambitions of becoming a truly national competition, it never truly expanded from its southern heartland. The towns of mid and north-west Wales were small and unlikely to be able to sustain professional teams, and in any event were difficult to get to from the south. In contrast, links with towns and cities in the south of England were good, and the crowds lucrative. Culturally, the larger conurbations had more in common with their English counterparts than with their rural compatriots. These trends were emphasised when the Football League expanded by swallowing the Southern League's senior teams, thus making fixtures against the top clubs in the English game feasible. Similar considerations led to the teams of the north joining competitions just across the English border, with Wrexham eventually being assimilated into the old Third Division North.

By introducing the national league the FAW were attempting to re-invent the social and sporting history of the 20th century. In many respects, little had changed in terms of the forces that had originally shaped Welsh club football. Transport links between north and south remained poor, there being no modern fast road, while rail links had largely disappeared in the 1960s. The towns of rural Wales remained unlikely to be able to sustain professional teams. Meanwhile, the glamour of the big city clubs of England had increased in the age of television. There remained cultural differences between North and South.

Yet in other ways, Wales was a very different place as the 20th century grew to a close. The virtual extinction of heavy industry lessened the contrasts between the rural bulk of Wales and the former southern industrial belt that was slowly reverting to nature. A Westminster-based Conservative Government, for whom few in Wales had voted, landed the final fatal blows to heavy industry, with a consequent growth in low-key Welsh nationalism. Whereas devolution had been decisively rejected as recently as 1979, public opinion was now more evenly divided, resulting in the narrow referendum majority in favour of a Welsh Assembly by 1997. The advent of European Union funding encouraged many to speculate as to the viability of a more independent Wales in the framework of a federal Europe. If transport infrastructure remained poor, modern cars and coaches did make journeys across the length of the country more viable. Television had provided a link between North and South that raised mutual awareness to levels unthinkable a century earlier.

However, whatever the changes in sense of nationhood, the reality was that the League of Wales in its initial form was to feature a series of semi-professional teams, often from smaller rural towns playing before crowds of a few hundred in facilities that were frequently spartan. This was hardly a glamorous set up, and it was difficult to see that it could defy the lessons of history and sustain professionalism. The Welsh FA tacitly admitted this when excusing Swansea, Cardiff and Wrexham from initial membership. The League of Wales was another world as compared to even the English Second and Third Divisions, let alone the increasing allure of the Premier League. As far as the "Big Three" clubs and the majority of their fans were concerned, the League of Wales was neither an attractive nor viable option. On the face of it, even allowing for the carrot of Europe, there was little to persuade the doubters that the status quo should be abandoned.

However, the changes wrought by time were not limited to internal events in Wales. The politics of football in England had also moved on apace. The original concept of the Premier League had been found in the Football Association's *Blueprint for Football* that envisaged the English structure moving in line with most of Europe with only the top two divisions being organised on a national basis, and the lower divisions being reorganised into a regional pyramid system. Whether the envisaged structure could have sustained professionalism below the top two divisions had been widely debated, but the issue became even more exaggerated when the proposals were hi-jacked by the larger clubs.

The formation of the Premier League and its associated television deals and revenues was to revolutionise the top division, and create a widening gap with the rest of the structure. It was unsurprising that over the next few years a series of schemes were put forward to create a second tier of the Premier League with a view to narrowing the divide. The net result of such plans would inevitably place the lower divisions on a worse financial footing, while there were also suggestions of ending automatic promotion and relegation between the second and third tiers. If such proposals became reality then it would be extremely difficult, if not impossible for clubs outside the original chosen elite to climb the league ladder to the very top.

At that stage neither Swansea City nor Cardiff City could be confident that they might receive an invitation to the exclusive party. Both clubs had achieved little on the field in recent years whilst their infrastructure was threadbare. In many respects the fortunes of both clubs had traced that of the local economy and were reflected in their financial struggles. The mooted solutions seemed to be limited to hoping that a passing millionaire would take a shine to either club. History was to show how uncertain an approach this could be. If the vision of an "elite forty" became reality, both Swansea City and Cardiff City faced a very real prospect of being left to wend their way in regional leagues from whence there was no automatic upward escape.

At the same time, European football was assuming a far greater importance. What once was exotic was fast becoming commonplace as the expanded Champions League appeared live on television on a regular basis. Even foreign league action was now readily accessible, and the stars of Milan and Real Madrid were becoming as familiar to British audiences as the major names of the Premier League. Meanwhile the ambitions of the major clubs of England became increasingly Europhile.

Few would seriously pretend that the League of Wales as it stood would be an adequate substitute for the Football League. History was certainly against such a concept. However, the world was changing. If the majority of Football League clubs were to be channelled into a permanent backwater in England with little chance of advancement, might the alternative of a revamped Welsh League with direct access to increasingly lucrative European competition be a more attractive alternative? If Swansea City were to find themselves facing a glass ceiling into the putative English elite, was it better to develop with an eye to the fast developing European alternative?

Too many of the real issues facing both the Football League clubs and their relationship with the League of Wales were not given a balanced debate. The reality for Swansea City in the mid-1990s was that they were playing in a league considered an anachronism by many of those who were now pulling strings in the corridors of power of modern English football. Meanwhile, hanging on by a thread to membership of the English professional structure was doing little to attract a disinterested local public. Such talk may have been unpalatable to many Swansea City fans, but the club's tenure in the upper reaches of the English structure was now history. Traditionalists may have wrung their hands, but the reality was that the world was changing, and the old certainties could no longer be taken for granted. The past was literally a different country.

That the League of Wales as it stood was not a suitable place for a top class professional team was almost certainly true. Whether Swansea City, or any of the 'big three', could any longer be described as a top class professional club that was able to sustain any worthwhile future within the English structure was a much more difficult question to answer.

*   *   *

If lack of positive direction had run through much of the club's history like lettering in rock, Swansea City's 1994-95 season was ultimately unable to break the mould. League form was again to result in a mid-table finish despite some good football, while fans drew most hope from cup runs. This time there was no trophy, but at least a visit was made to another of British football's great citadels.

As with the previous summer, anticipation had been high amongst the faithful as the new season approached, but doubt and disillusion had taken over by the time the first ball was kicked. Fans could be forgiven for believing that the previous year's success at Wembley had created enough interest in the City to encourage Doug Sharpe to strengthen the team for the promotion push that had failed to materialise 12 months earlier. The current squad had shown themselves capable of good football, and the basic framework of a decent side was present. If a target man and goalscorer could be added then surely the team could turn all that possession and neat approach play into goals and results.

The positive side of the build up to the new campaign was that there were no major departures, and that in particular Jason Bowen remained in a white shirt. The down side was that there were no major inward signings either. While David Penney, Kwame Ampadu and Michael Basham had been added in the second half of the previous season, there was no sign of the elusive striker that was surely the key to success. Questions were inevitably asked as to where goals would come from, as neither Steve Torpey nor Andy MacFarlane looked like creating too many scoring records

From the off, these doubts were confirmed as the side struggled to score, particularly at home. Two months into the season there had been only two goals registered at the Vetch in six matches, and a failure to record a single home win. The second of those goals was scored by John Hendry, brought in on loan from Tottenham, who hit the net five times in 10 matches in the league and Autoglass Trophy. Although far from the finished article, Hendry kick-started the home season into life with the first goal in a 2-0 win over Peterborough in late October.

The team owed a comfortable mid table position to some fine away results including wins at Hull, Cambridge and Crewe. The frustration of fans at the lack of a goal-scorer to turn the home draws into wins resulted in some appalling gates – only around 2,700 turned up to witness the Peterborough win. Discontent with the Sharpe regime was growing, and patience had worn thin with the chairman's mantra of his having saved the Swans. Fans perceived a club that was lacking positive direction. There was a feeling that if some forward impetus was not found, Swansea City could soon start to roll backwards. That the team only seemed one or two players short of being genuine promotion contenders only added to the frustrations. Inevitably, whether fair or not, comparisons were being made with Huddersfield, who seemed to have used their Wembley appearance as a springboard to better things, and were pushing for promotion at their shiny new 'state of the art' stadium.

Ironically league form became brighter in the gloom of November and December as six wins in eight starts coincided with success in the FA Cup that took the club to the third round. The first round tie at Walton and Hersham was remarkable for the thick fog that veiled the ground in the second half, almost completely obscuring the far goal from the view of the hardy Swans fans on the terrace behind Roger Freestone's net. Fortunately the Swans were wearing the almost luminous 'petrol pump' away kit, whose resemblance to council road-men's jackets at least made the players more visible. Not that this helped when the Swans' second goal went in. While it was possible to see celebrating players ghoulishly emerging from the eerie mist, the identity of the scorer was unknown to supporters until relayed by bush telegraph by the players back down the pitch and across the running track.

Grim weather also characterised the third round tie against Middlesbrough at the Vetch. John Ford proved an unlikely scorer with a 30 yard daisy cutter that seemed to skid into the corner of the net in a manner reminiscent of the Dambusters' bouncing bomb. If a popular television commercial of the time was to be believed, Boro keeper Kevin Miller had clearly been drinking the wrong sort of lager. Bryan Robson's side rallied to equalise, but the Swans should have sealed victory when Steve Torpey also failed to read the bounce of a cross when unmarked in the final minutes.

At that stage most fans were resigned to the cup run ending in the Ayresome Park replay, but a fine performance of no little skill and judicious riding of luck saw Torpey make amends to give the Swans a half time lead. Dave Penney doubled the advantage early in the second half, and despite 'Boro cutting the arrears and putting on late pressure, the boys in glowing orange held out for a memorable win. With Newcastle beating Blackburn in the following night's replay, a visit to Kevin Keegan's bar code army was the reward.

Around 3,000 Swans fans made the long trek north to enjoy what was increasingly likely to be a rare visit to a Premiership stadium. While St James' Park was developing into something of an unbalanced architectural mess, it certainly looked impressive from the city centre, a citadel high on a hill, glowing with a near celestial light on a gloomy late January afternoon in North East England. The one time darling of Kevin Keegan's resurgent team, Andy Cole, had left for Old Trafford, and the Toon Army were less than convinced by his cut-price replacement, Paul Kitson. Swansea defenders were in no position to join the chorus of sceptics, however, as Kitson scored a hat-trick. The make-weight in the Cole deal, Keith Gillespie, also gave Jon Ford a torrid afternoon.

However, the opening half had been a relatively even affair with both Martin Hayes and Steve Torpey having chances which if taken might have rattled the Geordies. As it was, those members of the Jack Army who had travelled for the weekend had to be content with a night on the Toon, and consoled themselves that at least that part of the day was the more pleasant for a home win.

Hayes' miss before the Gallowgate End was uncharacteristic, as he had scored a spate of goals during mid-season, including a classic chip over the goalkeeper in the Autoglass Trophy win at Oxford. There seemed a very real prospect of a return to Wembley to defend the Trophy, and the Wednesday after the trip to Tyneside saw the Swans appear before another bumper crowd at St Andrews to take on Birmingham. For the first time since the Toshack era the team played successive matches in front of 20,000-plus crowds. Sadly, the home side again scored three times, although the Swans had on this occasion scored twice to force the tie into extra-time where they fell to a golden goal. With the final appearance in the Welsh Cup ending with a 1-0 aggregate semi-final defeat by Cardiff City, the possibility of winning a further cup disappeared.

Happily, one precedent of the previous season had not been followed, and instead of limping into the Christmas period, the team hit form, and were handily placed in upper mid-table by the end of January. With the FA Cup run having apparently boosted funds, John Williams was borrowed from Coventry, where he had fallen out of favour. While not perhaps what most fans had envisaged, the Flying Postman did provide pace and physical presence. For the second time in the season, an on loan striker boosted performances, emphasising what many supporters saw as an obvious truth – bring in a decent forward who could score a few goals and the play-offs were a genuine possibility.

The result was a run of one defeat in 11 games, including a triumphant return to St Andrews. Another notable performance came in a comeback from 3-1 down at Rotherham to draw, a game when Williams was particularly influential. However, the highlight for most fans was the 4-1 demolition of Cardiff City in the Vetch Field snow. As the team rose to sixth place, a play-off spot seemed there for the taking, a run made all the more creditable by the absence of John Cornforth through injury. However, Williams returned to Coventry, and no replacement was signed. Almost inevitably, the problem of scoring goals resurfaced as three successive away matches were lost without a goal being scored. Notwithstanding a fine 2-1 win at Oxford in the final away game, the team subsided to finish in 10th place.

Those who travelled to the city of dreaming spires were rewarded by the sight of Roger Freestone's first ever league goal. The team had developed a paranoia from the penalty spot, memorably missing twice in an otherwise routine win over Orient at the Vetch. Few who were at the Manor Ground will forget the sight of Roger hurtling down the field toward the goal behind which the Swansea support stood, pausing only briefly to ward off other would-be takers, and determined to show off his superior technique. As Roger lashed the ball past his Oxford counterpart to the joy (and relief) of his fan club, one sensed that there must have been something deeply therapeutic for a goalie to be given the freedom of attempting to break the net. Afterwards some of us began to wonder whether the teams overall goal scoring record might have been improved if Roger could have played up front all season.

However, for the third successive season the club's supporters were left feeling that an opportunity had again been missed, and that we had the basis of a decent side that was under-achieving due to a lack of goals. The FA Cup run had reminded many fans of better days, although in some senses had diverted attention from the main task of escaping the division. The optimists saw the cup run as providing funds from which the final pieces could be added to the jigsaw. Pessimists worried that time was marching on, and that another year had gone by without promotion. In the end the latter group were to be proved right, as the team were to leave the Second Division behind, but in a manner not even the most depressive fan could have envisaged.

*   *   *

If Welsh football was an arena of internal conflict and change in the 1990s, it was hardly alone. As the South African hosted World Cup approached in the summer of 1995, Welsh rugby was already well into an era of soul-searching and blood-letting. The run up to sanctioned professionalism had not been a happy one for the so-called 'national game' of Wales, which had plummeted into serious decline. The local club scene was in disarray, as a series of reorganisations failed to remedy falling standards on the pitch and shrinking crowds off it. The Welsh national team's diminished status was confirmed in South Africa when for the second successive tournament they failed to progress beyond the group stage of the World Cup.

The source of these problems and their possible causes is not the subject of this book, and would probably fill several volumes by itself. Yet such is the perceived importance of rugby union to the sporting scene in South Wales that the potential knock on effects of this change on Welsh football and Swansea City in particular cannot be overlooked. Does the apparent decline of rugby union in Wales represent a historic opportunity for Welsh football?

Certainly it cannot be doubted that rugby union held a central place in Welsh identity in the 20th century. To outsiders, Wales was synonymous with the oval ball game, while domestically the successes of the national team and its succession of world-class players were a source of great pride. This inevitably had a knock-on effect on the local football clubs, including the Swans who by the 1970s were re-arranging home fixtures to avoid head-to-head competition with televised rugby internationals. Even during the Toshack era, the Swans could not necessarily feel confident of pulling in the crowds if there was the alternative attraction of a televised rugby clash from Cardiff Arms Park. In many quarters it is taken as read that competition from the 'dominant' sport of rugby has had an adverse effect on Welsh football, and in particular on the Swans. It certainly can be argued that the Welsh professional clubs have underachieved, and that Swansea City and Cardiff City might have become akin to Newcastle and Sunderland if football had been recognised as the 'national' game.

Yet beneath the national stereotyping and the pride in the successes of the Welsh team, the reality of sport in Wales was rather more complex. Was rugby union quite the article of faith as was generally portrayed? Certainly, when one takes Wales as a whole, the idea of rugby union being the 'national' game is questionable. Outside South Wales the game generally comes second to football. Even in rugby's heartlands, the level of participation in football is huge. Walk around the playing fields of a 'rugby hotbed' such as Llanelli on a Saturday afternoon, and the chances are that you will see as many if not more games of football in progress than rugby. Swansea has reputedly the largest amateur league in any English or Welsh city other than London and Birmingham. Is or was rugby quite as dominant a phenomenon in Wales as its supporters proclaim?

Even during the golden era of Welsh rugby in the late 1960s and 1970s, the club scene was not quite the hotbed painted in some quarters. While a major clash between the powerhouses of Welsh rugby or the sometime pretenders would draw good crowds, many ordinary club games were not well attended. While comparative data is difficult to assess due to rugby's tradition of not making gate figures public, anecdotal evidence suggests that crowds at run-of-the-mill club rugby matches in Wales were solid rather than spectacular.

If the idea of Wales as a rugby nation is not quite as straightforward as reputation suggests, from where did this perception originate? As has been referred to in an earlier section of this chapter, rugby had arrived in South Wales with the West Country middle classes who became the founders and architects of the new industrial communities. Sport was central to this sense of civic society but professionalism frowned upon. Amateur rugby was encouraged amongst the middle classes whilst "soccer" with its growing professionalism was frowned upon. The Welsh 'ruling' classes were able to project their values, particularly through the early media. The so-called 'mine owners' paper', *The Western Mail,* enthusiastically backed the oval ball game in its early years, endorsing the public school values of the early protagonists of South Wales society. While these local establishment forces were able to largely maintain amateur rugby's status within the area, they were however not able to wholly suppress the growth of football, and the two games seemed to eventually reach an uneasy accommodation.

Welsh rugby established hegemony on the back of continual success against the other home nations, and in particular the celebrated victory over the All Blacks in 1905. Success is central to any nation's self-esteem, and as long as victories could be obtained regularly, a sense of national identity and well being could be engendered. Throw in the regular success over the 'old enemy' of England and perhaps it is little wonder that rugby was seen as an appealing national 'success'.

Later on, the growth of the Welsh broadcast media, an industry inevitably dominated by the values of the Welsh middle classes, coincided with the second of Welsh rugby's golden eras. There seemed to be a historic meeting of these two forces, and rugby internationals became a truly national event as the thrilling exploits of a successful Welsh team were relayed across the country into increasing numbers of living rooms.

In contrast, the football team played against England and Scotland teams playing what was unequivocally the national game of those countries. With smaller numbers to select from it was always likely to enjoy rather less spectacular results. For all the great football players produced by Wales over the years, it is a small nation, and lasting success in a truly World game would always be a struggle. Even Wales sole appearance in the World Cup finals occurred before television coverage had percolated into most households.

Moreover, while the televised coverage of sport from the 1960s onward emphasised the successes of the Welsh rugby team, it also led to a new phenomenon, the television football fan. From the start of broadcasts of *Match of the Day*, there was no lack of interest in football among the Welsh public, but the underachieving Welsh clubs did not feature in the programme on a regular basis. The prospective spectator now could watch the best in Britain, albeit second hand. The public became choosy, and loyalty to the local team could no longer be taken for granted. Potential spectators could now watch the likes of Manchester United and Liverpool for free on television, and many saw no reason to waste good money on local mediocrity.

Had both Swansea Town and Cardiff City been in the old First Division during this era they would have attracted better television coverage and almost certainly been viewed more sympathetically by an increasingly media influenced public. While Swansea, Llanelli or Cardiff rugby clubs could reasonably claim to be platforms for the best rugby players in Britain, too often the Welsh football clubs became seen as also-rans. The chickens of wasted opportunity of the Swans in the 1950s came home to roost. The club had attracted large gates to see a team that many believed could have developed into one of the finest in Britain. Instead, the club was content with mediocrity, and perhaps it was little surprise that the public turned their back on the team in droves in favour of a game and clubs that offered the prospect of genuinely high-class entertainment. By the time the Swans did deliver under Toshack, the mould had already been set. The enforced decline of the 1980s merely exacerbated the problem, which was not necessarily lack of interest in football in Wales, but lack of incentive to support the local teams.

Yet by the mid-1990s the landscape had changed radically. The old industrial world around which the culture of Welsh club rugby had been built had largely disappeared. The national rugby team, no longer perceived as winners, were as likely to be a source of national embarrassment as of pride. The obvious lack of quality had led to a decline in interest in the club game. A series of changes to the domestic structure had generally failed to reverse the trend.

Moreover, football was in the midst of a huge boom across Britain, fed by a hyperbolic media that had abandoned images of rioting crowds in favour of the glamour and cosmopolitan appeal of the Premiership and Champions League. Wales was entering a new era, and the lords of the new church were up for election. It seemed that in addition to a huge latent interest in football, there was a large constituency of disaffected floating sports fans who had abandoned rugby and were there to be persuaded as to where their future loyalties lay.

For a game that had played second fiddle to rugby in the Welsh media for too long, this seemed a historic opportunity. With increased crowds would come increased sponsorship and greater commercial potential. Already high levels of participation would surely increase, with more chance of convincing talented individuals that their future lay in football. Whereas famous 1970s rugby internationals Phil Bennett and Geoff Wheel had been on the Swans' books, but opted for the glamour of contemporary rugby, future generations of young players might think differently.

Yet this all rested on providing the public with a worthwhile product, and therein lay the problem. If a massive opportunity to tempt the uncommitted had been lost through a lack of ambition in the pre-television age, Swansea City were now showing similar characteristics when televised football was now a major counter attraction. The Swans had failed to hold their audience when attending a live match was the only way to experience regular football, losing out to a rival game that offered relative glamour and success. Was history about to repeat itself, and a club that seemed to lack any momentum lose out to the more glamorous representatives of its own game? If the threat of the floating fan preferring the charms of St Helens or Stradey Park was not as great, the new competition seemed to come from the occasional visit to Old Trafford or Highbury backed with easy access to live action via satellite television.

Unfortunately, in the mid-1990s Swansea City appeared ill equipped to either exploit a historic opportunity or to meet the challenges from across the border. In contrast to the revitalised stadia of the Premiership, a visit to the Vetch was a step back in time to a world of poor facilities and potential violence. On the pitch, the club would have to prove that it could move forward and provide a product that was attractive. The sporting allegiance of South West Wales appeared up for grabs. If Swansea City were to benefit they could not afford to revert to type and allow history to repeat itself. Positive energy was needed from somewhere, but in the summer of 1995 it was difficult to see from where.

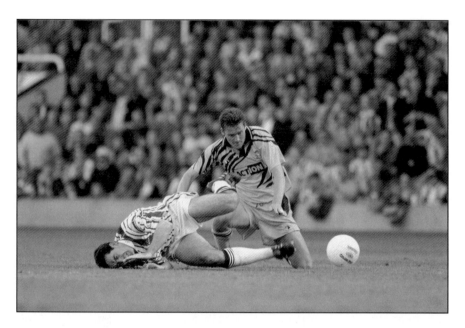

West Bromwich Albion versus Swansea – Football League play off May 1993
(Photo: Empics)

Newcastle United versus Swansea City, FA Cup 1995
(Photo: *South Wales Evening Post*)

Swansea City versus Huddersfield Town – Autoglass Trophy Final at Wembley
1994, the penalty shoot out. John Cornforth scores
(Photo: *South Wales Evening Post*)

Receiving the Autoglass Trophy at Wembley in 1994
(Photo: *South Wales Evening Post*)

Jan Molby after the 1997 play-off final
(Photo: *South Wales Evening Post*)

6.   Madness and embarrassment

The 1995-96 season was to realise the worst nightmares of those who felt that Swansea City was drifting along aimlessly. This season an ill wind blew the club onto a course toward the rocks. Yet nobody could have anticipated the unlikely twists that the story was to take over the following months. These were days when being a Swans fan meant putting a brave face on events whilst inwardly cursing those responsible.

If the previous close season had seen the playing staff remain un-ambitiously stable, 1995 saw the procession through the out door that fans had feared for some time. The most disappointing departure was that of Jason Bowen in a deal worth up to £350,000, particularly as his destination was Barry Fry's Birmingham City. Fry had embarked on a policy apparently designed to build the largest squad in the history of British football. The St Andrews club had a reputation not so much as sleeping giants but as perpetual somnambulists. Whatever their potential, it seemed likely that Bowen would become a squad player at a club that had become something of a graveyard of talent. Bearing in mind that, 18 months earlier, Bowen had been a reputed target for the likes of Newcastle, his eventual destination seemed an anti-climax.

If the rush to the exit had been Bowen's alone, fans may not have felt so concerned. However, the denuding of the rest of the squad raised real issues as to where the club was heading. Mark Harris, Jon Ford, Martin Hayes and Andy MacFarlane all left over the summer while Steve Jenkins was to leave by October. Harris in particular had, along with Keith Walker and Roger Freestone, been the defensive foundation of a team who had not found scoring easy. Jon Ford had just enjoyed his best season for the club, often deployed in a central defensive role, and while the fee of £200,000 represented a good return on a player whom many considered limited, a failure to recruit successors in central defence was worrying.

Again, Hayes and MacFarlane may have had their critics, but each brought something to the attack. For all his lack of pace, Hayes possessed a touch of genuine class and vision rare at Second Division level. Carl Heggs, a striker from West Bromwich Albion reserves, joined for £60,000, but was the sole recruit. For the first time in years the team appeared noticeably weaker on paper than the one that had finished the previous season. Once again, Frank Burrows was being asked to perform a minor miracle on a limited budget. There again, in another time and place, Doug Sharpe would have probably justified holding back expenditure on loaves and fishes – after all, far less than 5,000 attended the opening fixture.

Strangely, the season got off to a good start, with successive home wins over Shrewsbury (3-1), Peterborough (4-1) and Chesterfield (3-2) and a remarkable 2-2 draw at Bristol Rovers after the referee had somewhat harshly reduced the Swans to nine men by sending off Torpey and Heggs. However, the first indication that all was not well came in the second leg of the League Cup tie at Peterborough where a three goal cushion was overturned.

The Chesterfield victory had left the Swans in second spot in the germinal table, but it soon became evident that second from bottom was a far more likely finishing place. A 4-1 defeat at Walsall emphasised the side's defensive weaknesses, and players who a few months earlier had shown promise were suddenly looking like liabilities. Michael Basham had seemed a typically astute Burrows capture when he had joined the club, but now looked increasingly unsteady without Harris at his side, while the youthful Christian Edwards looked in danger of being over exposed too soon in a brittle team.

Those of us who suspected that all was not well behind the scenes had our suspicions confirmed when Frank Burrows announced his resignation following a 3-0 defeat at Burnley. Despite Doug Sharpe's protestation of shock, many fans felt that there was an inevitability about the decision, bearing in mind the distinctly bad vibrations emanating from Glamorgan Terrace over the summer. Rather than betrayed, most fans felt empathy with a manager who was seen as having done his utmost to build a decent team, yet had seen it dismantled by outward transfers.

The less committed public had already pre-empted Frankie by abandoning the team in droves as gates fell toward a level not seen since the traumas of the mid-1970s. In one sense change had been on the cards since the summer exodus, and most fans hoped that another wheeler-dealer could be found to turn matters around. Little were we to know the chain of events that was to evolve from Frankie's departure.

The chairman had made the club available for sale as anti-Sharpe sentiment grew more acute. The mantra of financial soundness was all very well, but to fans who could see that matters were fast unravelling on the pitch this was of little consolation. Burrows was replaced by his assistant Bobby Smith, and the change initially appeared to have some effect as the team produced its best performance of the season to dispatch promotion hopefuls Bradford 2-0 at the Vetch. Loan signings Robbie Dennison and Frank Lampard junior – whose first league game and goal, a prelude to bigger things elsewhere, were for the Swans - seemed to lift the side and eight points from five matches briefly saw the club climb the table. Most of us hoped for a season of mid-table mediocrity until the ownership question could be resolved.

Then the roof fell in, as Micky Adams' Fulham side blasted seven goals without reply in an FA Cup first round tie in a performance as craven as the nearby Cottage. For the faithful who had braved the open away end on a cold wet afternoon this had to rank amongst the 'worst ever' experiences as a Swansea fan. Supporters of clubs like the Swans are normally a stoical bunch who will be relatively philosophical in defeat as long as there is a feeling that the team has done its level best. Sadly, that afternoon by the chilly Thames the team degenerated into a rabble. Bobby Smith was living on borrowed time.

Doug Sharpe subsequently fell out with Smith over payment for training boots, both refusing to pay for new gear and sacking his manager as Christmas was nigh. Whatever the merits of the dispute, what was certain was that the team's form had continued where it left off at Fulham, with heavy defeats at Crewe, Oxford and at home to Burnley. Fans began to speculate as to whether the goals against column would reach record levels by the season's end. Eleven years earlier Doug Sharpe had made a brave decision just before Christmas when replacing Colin Appleton with John Bond, a decision that probably saved the club from relegation that season. This time there was to be no big name appointment to give hope going into the New Year. Jimmy Rimmer took over as caretaker, but without the ownership situation being resolved it was difficult to see that matters would improve overnight.

As Sharpe now openly courted buyers, some supporters began to get carried away with what proved to be ill-founded excitement as to the potential identity of the new owner. This was supposedly the era of the benevolent millionaire owner, who would mystically transform the fortunes of a struggling football club. Every 'sleeping giant' in the country, not to mention a few miscast pygmies, sought a figure like Jack Walker, who had transformed small town Blackburn. Some supporters fantasised about a similar figure changing the lives of the Cinderella Swans, although such dreams tended to ignore the sombre reality.

Multi-millionaires from South West Wales who had a genuine love of the club were thin on the ground. The super-rich owner can be a fine thing if they happen to be genuine supporters like Jack Walker or Elton John. However, where no such figure exists the net has to be cast wider, and one was then bound to question the motivation behind somebody with no immediate passion for the Swans becoming involved. Financial speculation, wild egotism and quaint eccentricity are three reasons that spring to mind, but are not qualities that will necessarily be good for a club. As Crystal Palace found to their cost under the infamous Mark Goldberg, even a genuine millionaire who is also a real fan can precipitate disaster if common sense is abandoned.

Eventually it was announced that the club was to be sold to one Michael Thompson, a West Midlands millionaire with little apparent natural connection to the club. While some members of the local media began to speculate imaginatively on the identities of potential recruits as new manager, many of us anticipated that the reality would be rather more prosaic. Nobody anticipated the depth of obscurity and consequent notoriety that we were about to plunge.

Thompson revealed that Swansea City's new manager was to be one Kevin Cullis, then in charge of the Cradley Heath youth team. The portly Cullis, had never been employed in any credible professional football context. Years later, he was to be convicted for his part in a fraud. For Swansea City fans he had already perpetrated a huge scam merely by turning up to work at the Vetch. The best that can be said of Cullis's reign at the Vetch was that it was short. In reality it lasted two and a half matches, by which time the players had decided that senior professional Dave Penney would take the interval team talk. Cullis's position was untenable, and so by extension was Thompson's. However unpopular Doug Sharpe had been before, his return to pull the plug on the sale drew sighs of relief. The devil we knew had never been as welcome.

Ironically, the Thompson administration's one positive act was to interest Liverpool's Danish midfielder Jan Molby in joining the Swans. Why such a skilful player wished to be associated with such a farcical regime was anybody's guess. Whatever the reason, Molby appeared in the not inconsiderable flesh in the stand during Cullis's final home game in charge. Sharpe seized the opportunity, and within days of the Thompson sale collapsing, Molby was installed as the fifth manager of the season.

Whatever else the Swans could be accused of in what had become a surreal season, ringing the changes could not be on the charge sheet. During early 1996 most supporters opened the sports pages with trembling fingers, hopeful that some new indignity had not been foisted on the club. Whatever the reservations of appointing a rookie manager in a difficult situation on the pitch, employing Molby did at least make the Swans seem like a serious football club once more.

Inevitably, parallels were drawn with the appointment of a certain Mr Toshack, but aside from the obvious Liverpool connection, the circumstances couldn't have been more contrasting. Toshack had inherited a recovering club featuring some exciting young talent who stood well positioned in a promotion race with the final stretch in sight. Molby had come into a club that was distinctly wobbly off the pitch, and whose confidence-drained journeymen were staring relegation in the face.

The Dane's arrival at least lifted spirits and three successive home wins and three away draws suggested that a great escape might still be in the script. Sharpe made money available and Molby signed defender Shaun Garnett and attackers Lynton Brown and Colin MacDonald, while the experienced striker Lee Chapman joined on a short-term deal. Meanwhile, John Cornforth joined Jason Bowen in Birmingham's cast of dozens.

Once again, however, the pattern of the season recurred as early promising results under a manager degenerated into a number of heavy defeats. This time the wheels came off in the second half at Valley Parade, where the scoreless first half turned into a 5-1 defeat, care of a crazy quarter of an hour when Bradford scored four times. The second half defending was as shambolic as anything seen previously in the season. A 3-1 defeat by Wrexham at the Vetch left the club reliant on the failure of others, and despite successive wins over Brighton and Wycombe, relegation was made official with a 4-0 defeat at Notts County in the penultimate game. Swansea City were back in the division they had left some eight seasons before. At that time it was called the fourth and was now officially the third, but no amount of re-branding could make it sound more attractive.

For the fans, the worst aspect of this season when disaster masqueraded as farce was that it all seemed so avoidable. Substantial money had come into the club from outward transfers and sell-on deals, and even allowing for low gates, past losses and future provision there still seemed to be no rhyme or reason to the transformation from play-off hopefuls to prime relegation fodder. To make the situation even more frustrating, money was suddenly made available when it was arguably too late. One can only speculate as to what might have happened if the sums made available to Molby had been made available to Frank Burrows months earlier. Certainly one could guess that money would have been better spent, for none of the inexperienced Molby's signings at that stage proved good long-term acquisitions. Further, was it fair to either Molby or the club to throw him into such deep waters without experienced assistance in his first managerial job? Did we need an old hand at the helm, if only until the season's end? Such questions occurred to fans who were powerless to influence the tragi-comic soap opera that had played over the previous nine months. All are imponderables, but fans had every right to feel aggrieved.

Over the years, Swansea fans have had to learn to accept both success and failure as impostors with equal grace. This time around however, the situation seemed to have been avoidable. Relegation was one thing, but seeing the club descend into shambles was another. Those who tried to see the glass as half full took strength from Molby's presence, and hoped for better things next season. Those who saw it as half empty could see little respite while the club remained in its current ownership. Yet as experience had shown, finding credible new owners with the club's interests at heart was not as easy as some people liked to imagine. Football was changing, but Swansea City showed every indication of being left behind in the scramble.

*   *   *

For most fans the turning point and single determinant factor in what had become a *season horriblis* was the moment when Frank Burrows decided to walk away. After all, this was a manager who had brought a degree of success, and more importantly, stability. Compared to the managerial musical chairs that had bedevilled other parts of the Sharpe era, Frankie represented continuity.

Burrows had arrived at a club that had been rocking dangerously during Terry Yorath's second spell in charge, and he immediately steadied the ship and saw off the threat of relegation with a little to spare. Yorath had provided an eloquent personification of the adage 'never go back', the success of his first term being forgotten among recriminations over the manner of his departure and the inconsistency of results during his second tenure. Burrows stopped a nasty decline before slowly rebuilding the team.

As a manager he will probably best be remembered as the great uncoverer of talent in unlikely places, and his transfer record was one of the most impressive in the club's recent history. During his first close season in charge he splashed out all of £15,000 to bring John Williams and Jon Ford out of the Dr Marten's league. The pair were subsequently sold on for a total of £450,000. Later on Des Lyttle was to make a journey from Worcester City to Nottingham Forest via the Vetch, netting the Swans a major profit along the way.

Frank's list of signings for the club spoke for itself. In addition to Williams, Ford and Lyttle he brought in John Cornforth, Dave Penney, Kwame Ampadu and Steve Torpey, all of whom either gave solid service or were sold at a substantial profit. He successfully handed veterans such as Martin Hayes and Colin West a lifeline (even if the latter didn't appreciate the gesture) while also bringing along young players such as Jason Bowen and Steve Jenkins.

On the pitch Frank took a team that had been relegation candidates for three seasons in a row and built them into one of the better teams in the division, playing neat passing football in accordance with the club's best traditions. A Second Division play-off spot, the Autoglass Trophy, and an FA Cup run represented the club's most successful period since the demise of John Toshack.

Sadly, this relative success on the pitch was not reflected in the club's attendances. Some might argue that there was a perception that the club wasn't scoring enough goals and winning regularly enough at home to be genuine contenders, and pointed to Frank's preferred formation with a lone man up front. However, the reluctance of the West Wales public to get behind the team may have had deeper roots, themselves possibly the cause of Frank's ultimate disillusion.

Whatever public face he may have put on matters, the suspicion was that Frank Burrows became frustrated for exactly the same reasons as the fans. Running a tight ship with limited finance and suffering the odd sale was one thing. Continually having to rebuild was another. The summer of 1995 had seen various key departures including Jason Bowen, probably the club's most promising young player. Frank may have felt that having built some decent foundations, he might have been allowed to strengthen and develop the team. Instead he found that it was to be weakened and that he would have to start again. Few fans could really blame him for having had enough – so had most supporters.

History will surely judge Frank Burrows as one of the better Swansea managers. Many supporters believe that if he had been given more in the way of support by the board, relegation would never have entered the equation. He might have constructed a squad good enough to make the play-offs or even win promotion. The club has never come so close to that level since. Ultimately, in the absence of such a feat, he will be remembered as a classic lower league wheeler-dealer and scout of talent, with an ability to build a good team on limited means.

In the final analysis Frank seemed to see the writing on the wall, and moved on rather than fall victim to a changing football world that was to be distorted by wage-inflation, and a club that seemed ill-equipped to live with the times. Certainly Frank never deserved the insulting songs disrespectfully sung about him by sections of the North Bank with short memories when he became manager of Cardiff City some years later. What he did deserve was more support from both the board and the city at large. Some would say the latter was dependant on the former.

*   *   *

If most of the 1995-96 season and its eventual outcome were to be the cause of gloom and despondency amongst Swansea City fans, at least some were able to find a positive distraction over the following summer when the European Championships were held in England. Hosting the event symbolised England's rehabilitation within European football following the dark days of the late 1980s, and provided a further boost to the domestic image of the game in the new tele-visual football age. If the World Cup of 1990 had turned around the wider public's view of football, the 1996 tournament was the moment when the new relationship was reinforced as the love affair between the media and football intensified.

If football was coming home in England, then in Wales it had gone on extended leave. Unlike in 1994, Welsh football fans couldn't even claim that the national side had come close to qualifying. Following the controversial decision not to renew manager Terry Yorath's contract, the side had gone into serious decline under the stewardship of first Mike Smith and later Bobby Gould. From being the nearly men, Wales developed into little more than cannon fodder as a disastrous qualification campaign for Euro 96 was followed by an equally embarrassing attempt to qualify for the 1998 World Cup.

For Swansea City fans there was a depressing sub-plot to these failures. The build up to Euro 96 had seen a significant event in the relationship between the Swans and the Welsh team. During the qualifying match against Germany at Cardiff Arms Park in October 1995, Steve Jenkins became the last player to come through the Vetch Field youth system to appear in a competitive international match for Wales while a Swansea player. While both Chris Edwards and Roger Freestone were to subsequently appear for Wales, their appearances were in friendly matches. In any event, while a great club stalwart, Roger was not a Swans product.

For a club that had a history as a production line of talent, this was a depressing trend. This was particularly so bearing in mind the depths plumbed by the Welsh team over the next few years. When Bobby Gould resorted to picking players from lower division sides such as Bristol Rovers and Crewe, but not from Swansea, it seemed a poor testimony to the Swans youth system. From talents such as the Allchurch brothers, Cliff

63

Jones, Mel Charles and Terry Medwin in the 1950s, through Alan Curtis, Robbie James and Jeremy Charles in the 1970s to Andy Melville and Chris Coleman in the 1980s and 90s, the Swans had contributed a stream of players to the Welsh team.

Indeed, so *blasé* were the club about the wealth of local talent at its disposal, that they became quite generous in sharing it with other clubs. The Swans have the dubious distinction of having allowed at least three players who went on to become established international players slip through their fingers. John Charles, Giorgio Chinaglia and Dean Saunders were all deemed good enough to be stars at Juventus, Lazio and Aston Villa respectively, but not it seems the Swans. If the real stories behind the departure of this trio are a little more complex, their mere presence on the club's books is indicative of the talent that was once recruited.

Moreover, it seems odd that whereas historically the club had produced exciting attacking players, that the more recent alumni of the Vetch academy had been in the main defenders. Was the Swansea area no longer producing good quality players, and in particular skilled attackers? Were the club simply missing out on the talent available? Or was there something wrong with the way the club was developing the talent that was on its books?

Certainly Swansea and South Wales are very different places to the way they were in the 1970s, let alone the 1950s. Some would say that the loss of the close-knit industrial culture has led to different leisure patterns for children, and young players develop in a different way. Certainly there is an argument that when players rise out of a background of material poverty with the most basic of facilities that they seem to exhibit a joyfulness in play that is not always evident in more affluent cultures. Many of the world's greatest entertainers and ball players emerged from the back streets or the mud pitch with bundles of rags at their feet. Did the shanty towns of Sao Paulo and Buenos Aires have something in common with the terraces of the Swansea Valley? Where lives are tough is there a greater urge to leaven the day-to-day grind through flashes of genuine inspiration?

While there may be something to such theories, it is easy to get sucked into the sepia romance of sweaters as goalposts and the past being a mythical golden place. One can hardly suggest poor nutrition and deprivation of facilities as a recipe for the development of young players in the modern world. In any event, the French and Dutch appear to have little difficulty in reconciling modern affluent society with the production of exciting and skilled players. Add in the fact that the Swansea area is one of the poorest in Western Europe, and the shortcomings of such theories are exposed.

It would also not be true to say that there have been no young players of promise to emerge from the Swansea and West Wales areas in recent years. Welsh internationals such as John Hartson, Simon Davies, Mark Delaney and Matthew Jones have all emerged from what the Swans might think of as their natural geographic constituency, but signed for other clubs. Promising Swansea schoolboys such as James Thomas and Chris Llewellyn also disappeared over Offa's Dyke as trainees. Is the real issue one of effective scouting rather than dearth of talent?

Yet the loss of good young players is hardly a new phenomenon. John Charles was one of a line of local players including Gary Sprake, Carl Harris and Matthew Jones who were snapped up by Leeds, while Leighton James and Brian Flynn went to Burnley. There was a period in the 1960s when the club's scouting system appeared to fall apart, but the damage was made good in the 1970s. However, as the decade wore on, Swansea fans could be forgiven for wondering whether there had been a similar lapse in the 1990s.

Over the coming seasons under both Jan Molby and John Hollins, a number of young players were given an opportunity, but the majority fell by the wayside, and there was a feeling that the Swans had missed out on the best of young local talent. This is not to denigrate the individuals involved in the club's youth development programme. The head of the youth development team, Mal Elias, was clearly well regarded, as was evidenced when he left for Premiership Southampton. Later on, Alan Curtis was to become part of the Welsh national set up. Were there greater forces at play, beyond the power of a club such as Swansea City?

It is certainly correct that competition for young talent has grown to a level wholly unrecognisable from the 1950s, when most youngsters joined their local club. Now dark rumours do the rounds of incentives offered to parents and youth coaches to guide youngsters toward the major clubs.

While it may not have attracted the attention of too many Swans fans at the time, West Ham caused something of a stir when in January 2000 they were ordered by an FA tribunal to pay £400,000 for 16-year-old Leon Britton who they had signed, despite him having been on Arsenal's books since he was 10 years old. Britton was to play his own part in the Swansea City story in the future, but his early history illustrates the lengths to which bigger clubs will go to capture latent talent.

Later the same year the same tribunal ordered Southampton to pay the Swans £100,000 for Gowerton-born Richard Jones after he signed professional forms for the Hampshire club, despite having been nurtured at the Vetch through his schoolboy years. In modern football one has to accept that a lower division club cannot compete in financial terms, and that if one of the big clubs comes calling, few youngsters would not have their heads turned, let alone be in a position to resist temptation. It used to be enough to persuade a young player to join his local club that he could live at home and get a fair crack at the first team at an early stage. Those now seem innocent times.

Yet Luton signed John Hartson, while Simon Davies went to Peterborough - neither could realistically be described as glamour clubs. Most Swans supporters would be stoical about losing promising local youngsters to Manchester United. However, young players' preference for clubs that are logically no bigger than the Swans inevitably prompts questions. Did the club overlook these players? If not, then why did they find the overtures of these rivals more attractive?

Swansea City has always had a history of developing good quality players. The continuation of this tradition is surely critical to both the future success of the club and its identity with the local community. Both the nearly team of the 1950s, and the core of the side successful under Toshack were built on products of the club's youth system. It is not unrealistic to believe that, if the club are once again to progress through the leagues, a nucleus of home-grown players will be crucial. Competition from elsewhere, plus question marks about the club's system meant that as the second half of the nineties began, this aspect of the club's tradition looked under threat.

7.   Danish blues

By the summer of 1996 it was clear that British football was changing beyond recognition. If England's successful hosting of Euro 96 was testimony to the rehabilitation of the country's football in international eyes following the shame of Heysel, matters had also moved apace in the domestic game. If the initial advent of the Premiership had seemed little more than a re-branding of an old product, four years on it was apparent that there had been developments that profoundly altered the whole ethos of British football.

Around the country new stadia and stands had appeared as clubs rushed to comply with the Taylor Report and the all seat requirements of the top two divisions. Foreign players were now commonplace rather than an exotic exception, attracted by lucrative wage packets that inflated in competition with ticket prices. A tangible gap was opening up between the Premier League and the top of the First Division, evidenced by the number of clubs who were relegated after their first season at the top. Many fans, not least from those clubs who were at the cutting edge of these changes, began to ask where all this was heading.

Some clue as to what the future might hold could be gleaned by looking across the Atlantic at American professional sports. Leading off-field figures in the English game such as Arsenal's David Dein pointed at the American major leagues as the benchmark for the marketing and presentation of football. In particular, the huge commercial success of American pro-football through the NFL was cited by Alex Fynn, deputy chair of the Saatchi and Saatchi advertising agency who contributed to the FA's *Blueprint for Football.*

In many respects the likes of Dein and Fynn were correct in their analysis that British football could not keep on the same road that it had travelled in the 1970s and 1980s. Change was necessary if football was to buck the trends of those decades. However, British fans – who had little say in what the movers and shakers decided – were entitled to ask whether the alternative direction was the right one. What was this American vision, and what were the likely effects on British football if it were to be achieved? More specifically in the context of this book, where would Swansea City stand if British football became the sporting equivalent of the 51st state?

It was easy to see the positive virtues of the American experience. Stadia and facilities were spectator friendly, while crowds were generally large with few behaviour problems. The marketing initiatives and television revenues generated made most British operations seem very small beer. Yet behind the veneer of success, the realities of the American scene were a little more complex. In particular there were a number of aspects that would surely not be welcomed by British football fans. Some had evolved in a specific American context and might not travel well if superimposed on a game that had a very different cultural and social background.

American Football had developed commercially in a very particular time and place, exploiting the expanding television market of the consumer boom post-War USA. Prior to the 1960s public attention on American football centred on the college games, while most of the clubs were semi-professional and played in regional leagues. The NFL effectively exploited the possibilities of the twin developments of television and jet airline travel to set up a national league. A child of the television age, the NFL recognised the desirability of ensuring genuine competition between all the teams. Starting with a virtually empty page, its founders were able to structure the competition to ensure relative equality, through both the draft system that encouraged equality of playing staffs, a central merchandising system and a relatively even distribution of the income generated.

Inherent to the concept was the idea of a fixed number of teams playing in a structure that had no promotion or relegation. The advantage from the owners' point of view was they were guaranteed a fresh start and a crack at the top teams every season, free from the business risks attached to relegation. On the other hand, a successful junior side could never progress to the ranks of the major leagues, unless there was an expansion of the leagues, meaning that they would always lose their better players to the major league teams.

American professional teams were unashamedly run as commercial franchises with the specific goal of making money for their owners. There was little room for sentiment or tradition in this world-view. This was perfectly illustrated in the summer of 1996 when the Cleveland Browns transferred their franchise to Baltimore, not because they were losing money, but because the governing authorities in the latter city simply put a more lucrative proposition on the table. This was hardly the first instance of an American team moving home because the financial grass was greener elsewhere. It seemed cities were prepared to enter auctions in order to secure the presence of a major league franchise. Team owners were the clear winners in this scenario, with loyal fans the greatest losers.

Indeed, the loyalty of fans appeared something of a low priority. Ticketing policies of the NFL appeared pitched toward those with a high disposable leisure income, with the less affluent left to watch on television. Whilst this might satisfy the accountants, it didn't necessarily enhance the live experience, as was illustrated by the New York Jets whose entire regular season in 1996 was officially sold out, but who recorded some 60,000 'no shows' for one of the final home games of an unsuccessful season. The sales figures represented economic success; the empty seats a complete lack of atmosphere.

There was little doubt that there were a number of aspects of American Football from which British football could usefully learn. However, there were a number of striking contrasts between the historic background of the NFL and that of British football that made one question whether the cultural borrowing was entirely appropriate.

Even the largest British football clubs have evolved out of their communities, often having origins in works teams or other social institutions such as churches. During the heyday of industrial Britain, teams had sprung up throughout the land, with the concept of advancement via promotion through the league system an inherent part of the culture. This development from grass roots is clearly a very different concept from setting up a series of commercial entertainment franchises with a mass television audience specifically in mind.

In some respects British football had more in common with another more traditional American sport – baseball – which had not had American Football's advantage of starting with a virtually blank page, and was suffering deep rooted problems as it attempted to adjust to the modern media dominated market. These difficulties were recognised when the national Commissioner ordered an in-depth report into the game's problems, published in 2000. The report found that an imbalance of income off the pitch had a direct correlation to success on it. Clubs such as the New York Yankees had built up huge historic followings, and the practice of individually marketing clubs had led to a few assuming dominant positions. Fans grew tired of a few teams having a virtual monopoly on the prizes. Other teams were spending beyond their means in order to keep up, with the result that many were trading at a loss. This had also led to massive wage inflation that in turn had led to increased admission charges. In some instances this had led to declining gates, and a threat to the concept of baseball being an affordable family sport. These concerns were to be echoed in British football in the new millennium.

Those who propounded the virtues of the NFL were less keen to trumpet the checks and balances of that system, including the relative equal distribution of income and centralised merchandising. It seemed that they wanted the 'benefits' without the elements designed to aid sporting competition. They were effectively endorsing the hybrid system that had developed within baseball that had been criticised by that game's own Commissioner's report.

In many respects the American system represents a more suitable blueprint for some form of Europe wide super-league more than it does as a panacea for the ills of domestic British football. This, of course may not be a million miles from the ambitions of some of the British clubs whose representatives were the loudest admirers of the American way. Yet if this particular vision were to become reality, then it is difficult to be optimistic about the place of Swansea City in the scheme of things. If Wales was to be represented in a pan-European club competition, Swansea City would have an uphill struggle to convince the power brokers that Cardiff as capital should not be the representative, leaving the Swans as a mere junior feeder club.

Even if the entrepreneurial dream of a money-spinning invitation

European super-league was some way off, there remained the alternative possibility of the drawbridge being raised within the domestic leagues. As was mentioned in an earlier chapter, plots were hatched in the following years by a collection of middle ranking clubs with a view to form an exclusive second league tier, designed to both close the financial gap with the Premiership but also to protect investment by denying automatic promotion to and from an elite of forty or so professional clubs. If any such glass ceiling were to be introduced, there had to be doubts as to whether the Swans would make the cut. Whatever the arguments over the club's potential, the playing record over recent years hardly put the Swans in the 'top 40.' If such a scheme were ever adopted, the whole future of Swansea City as a professional club might come into question.

Many would say that such schemes have been mooted in the past, but that nothing radical has actually happened. Yet in 1992 few fans would have thought that franchising would have any place in British football. Twelve years on, Wimbledon had metamorphosed into the MK Dons. During their deliberations on that issue the football authorities made it implicit that they placed the interests of business investors ahead of those of the club's fans. On recent form, it would be a brave person who would wager that the overall good of British football would win out in the future over commercial interests. If we have franchising today, who is to say that there might not be a closed shop tomorrow?

There are many troubling messages that emerge from the idea of British football emulating American sport. Whatever positive ideas might usefully be learned from across the Atlantic, it should always be borne in mind that the central philosophy of those teams is essentially that of commerce. This throws up fundamental questions as to how British fans perceive their clubs. There is, of course, an argument in support of the concept of a club being a commercial entity that provides entertainment to consumers who can take or leave what is on offer. However, one suspects that this is a view that would not be shared by a majority of British football fans. If supporters see their team as being a sporting institution and community organisation rather than purely a business that occasionally provides them with entertainment, then they should be wary of slavishly following the American model.

Yet ironically, if the adoption of American values has contributed to what many fans would see as problems for the British game, potential solutions and redemption can be found from a similar source. The USA provides one of the most stirring examples of supporters acting to ensure that their team does not become the pawn in an entrepreneurial game. Several years ago the owners and supporters of the Green Bay Packers football team became one and the same, setting up an elaborate shareholding scheme that guarantees the continued presence of the team in the modest Wisconsin city. For those who might dismiss this form of supporters' trust as idealistic nonsense that has no place in the viciously competitive world of professional sport, the Packers' record stands comparison with any of the teams owned by "entrepreneurs". Sound management by those who care combined with the relatively fair system of income distribution within the NFL has ensured that pro-football has endured successfully in a city that the profit-seeking businessman might have long abandoned.

Yet back in 1996, the supporters of Swansea City, together with those of many other clubs, were a long way from taking such lessons on board. The club had already sought a super-rich backer with embarrassing results. However, the search for, and many fans desire for an owner with economic clout continued unabated. Over the coming seasons the club would follow the example of many other British clubs and cease to be the personal property of local oligarchy and go down the road of becoming a commercial enterprise. In the event, the results were to be disastrous. Thankfully one example from the USA was still to indirectly provide the inspiration for salvation.

*   *   *

For most Swansea City fans the build up to the 1996-97 season was a time of mixed feelings. While Doug Sharpe had pulled the plug on the Thompson sale, the underlying fear remained that the ownership situation was far from stable. Moreover, following the Thompson fiasco it seemed the club and its supporters were stuck between a rock and a hard place. The fans had learnt the hard way that, millionaire or not, new owners did not necessarily come riding aboard white chargers. On the other hand, the club was still owned by a regime that many fans believed lacked what was needed to truly turn things around.

Equally, on the field, views were mixed as to the season's prospects. The arrival of Jan Molby had undoubtedly lifted sprits, and despite the previous season's eventual relegation, it would be interesting to see what the Dane could do with the team from a fresh start. Yet while Molby had brought a sense of confidence and purpose back to the club, the team was in unproven hands. It had lost its relegation battle from a position that was difficult but not impossible. While it would be unfair to blame Molby for the mess he inherited, some felt that he was too inexperienced to deal with a demanding situation and that an 'old head' would have been a better bet for both staving off the dreaded drop, and rebuilding the team.

Indeed it had to be said that Molby's signings of the previous season had hardly set the world alight. MacDonald appeared lightweight and ineffective, Brown fitful, while Shaun Garnett never settled and was soon to be on his way to Oldham where he was to give far better value than he did at the Vetch. The summer saw tricky winger John Hodge depart for Gillingham and Molby signed a youngster named Richie Appleby as his replacement. Most excitement was generated by the arrival of full back Joao Moreira from Benfica for £40,000.

Despite the encouragement of an opening day 2-1 win over Rochdale that featured a spectacular goal by Dave Penney, the early season results suggested that those who had predicted a struggle were correct. Would Molby follow the Bobby Charlton school of former great players turned managers, rather than that of John Toshack? Molby had been sent off against Rochdale, and as suspensions and injuries took their toll, he was forced to rely on younger players. While there was an encouraging 4-0 thumping of Hereford, limitations were exposed when league leaders Fulham won 2-1 at the Vetch in September.

With both the Swans and Cardiff City both struggling in the lower half of the Third Division, the future of Welsh club football within the English pyramid was not looking rosy. Neither club was well resourced, or could see a credible saviour on the horizon at that point. To add to the growing feeling of despair, September saw Doug Sharpe once again officially put the club up for sale, and with the team struggling on the pitch, a repeat of the previous season and the potential nightmare of losing Football League status beckoned.

By late October a series of draws and losses culminated in a 2-0 defeat at Torquay, leaving the team 20th in the league. It seemed the club was in terminal decline, and as autumn turned to winter, life was looking increasingly bleak. About the only bright thing about the club at that stage was the new Le Coq Sportif kit, which was felt by many fans to be the best in years, returning to a more traditional white and black kit after the various black and red waves, stripes and flashes that had adorned the famous white shirt in recent seasons.

Suddenly, without any apparent external catalyst, the form of the team turned dramatically. Whereas autumn had seen them unable to do anything right, winter was a complete contrast. Molby's anger following the Torquay debacle had the desired effect and a few days later promotion chasing Wigan were beaten 2-1 at the Vetch. This sparked a run of 13 matches in which only two were lost, and by the new year the Swans were in the play-off spots and hitting form that must have had the leading three looking nervously over their shoulders. Fulham, in particular had hit a difficult patch, and when the Swans went to Craven Cottage in February and led after an hour, the dream of automatic promotion remained very much alive. Unfortunately, the Londoners punished some less than tight defending to recover to a 2-1 win, and from that point onward never looked back.

The gap opened by the win proved unassailable, but one wonders what might have become of the two club's respective seasons had the Swans hung on. To say the least, the nerve of Micky Adams' Fulham team would have been tested. Instead, psychology seemed to play a different role, as with the top three well clear of the pack, the Swans appeared to accept that automatic promotion was not to be. As spring turned to summer, young men's hearts turned to the play-offs, and while the team's form didn't quite hit the heights of winter, qualification was settled with something to spare.

The team had at least attempted to play neat passing football, and at times succeeded to good effect. Molby's presence had obviously been crucial in certain games, as would any player of his pedigree and ability. When he was not available, senior players such as Penney and Ampadu had risen to the occasion. Up front, Steve Torpey showed that with support he could be an effective target man and leader of the attack at Third Division level. Young players such as Lee Jenkins, Jonathan Coates and Christian Edwards had also played important roles. The former two showed a degree of enterprise under Molby that seemed to go missing later in their careers, while Edwards filled the gap left by Garnett alongside Walker in the centre of defence. If his inexperience sometimes led to the occasional error, it was clear that he was growing into the role, and seemed set to emulate the likes of Andy Melville.

The play-offs initially pitted the Swans against Chester, thus avoiding Cardiff City in the semi-final, but also raising what for many fans was the dread prospect of a day out at Wembley that would be no fun whatsoever. While the Welsh media would doubtlessly have talked up the event, the reality was that a coach convoy along the M4 in scenes reminiscent of the miners' strike was hardly an enticing prospect. The thought of every psychopath in South Wales descending on north-west London hardly promised a jolly day out.

The Swans efficiently killed the away leg of the tie with Chester, a goal-less draw setting up a night of tension at the Vetch. With the crowd near the official capacity, the atmosphere evoked memories of promotion battles in the Toshack era. For fans who had stuck with the team during the previous season's humiliations, this was a welcome reward.

Yet, as so often happens when the crowd is large and expectant, the early stages were far from encouraging. Steve Jones, who had proved himself a brave and committed defender since his step up from semi-professional football was badly injured during an accidental clash in the Swans' penalty area. It became obvious that the injury was serious and that Jones would play no further part in the game. Little did we know the true extent of the injury as he was driven away in an ambulance that had been brought onto the pitch. In many ways it was a miracle that Jones ever wore the white shirt again. As it was he was out of the match, Wembley and football altogether for over a year. As play resumed several players seemed shaken. Might this turn of events undermine concentration?

Chester proceeded to shoot themselves in the foot by having a man sent off before half time, and the balance of the match tipped slightly in the Swans' direction. Molby's team took full advantage, as headed goals from Dai Thomas and Steve Torpey established a 2-0 lead at the interval. When Carl Heggs made it three in the second half the party really began, and the Swans could easily have doubled their score. The filtering news that Cardiff had lost to Northampton, and that the road to Wembley was not to become a war-zone for the day, added to the celebrations. Having failed to get to Wembley for 71 years, the Swans were now going for the second time in four seasons.

The day out at Wembley turned out to be a contrasting experience in almost every sense to the Autoglass Trophy. About the only thing in common was the glorious sunshine. The relative importance of the fixture meant that tension was higher. Most people regarded the Autoglass as a pleasant diversion, a day out at Wembley in which even defeat would have had its consolations. The play-offs were very different, for actual status depended on the outcome. Even before a ball was kicked, we knew that today mattered, and for all the talk of 'enjoying the day out', most hard-core fans knew deep down that we were in for a day on the rack.

Events on the field are well documented. The sides largely cancelled each other out, with few clear cut chances being created. Those who doubted Molby's chosen 4-3-3 formation before the match were vindicated. On Wembley's large pitch, and with a player-manager not noted for his mobility, the Swans' midfield was exposed. Yet even now it is hard to think of a more cruel way to end both a match and a season.

The sheer numbness of seeing John Frain's free-kick hit the back of our net just as we were resigning ourselves to extra time is something that no words can adequately express. For minutes afterwards Swans fans could be seen staring into space in bewilderment, not quite having taken in what they had just witnessed. To compare supporter reaction to that of witnesses to an accident would be to trivialise genuine tragedy, yet there did seem to be a collective sense of shock in the Swansea end. To concede in the final minute to a side that had rarely looked dangerous, and to a twice taken free kick seemed a particularly twisted script.

The result and its nature meant that hardly anybody in the Swansea contingent regarded the day at Wembley with any affection. As it was, once the initial shock had worn off, all we could do was to reflect that under Molby the team had come as close as was possible to regaining their previous status at the first attempt. The optimists believed that if the club could retain the core of the same team to start the following season, then surely the team should be challenging for automatic promotion. We had quite forgotten that this was Swansea City, and that expecting the future to evolve logically was futile.

*   *   *

The final whistle at Wembley brought to an end not only the dream of an immediate return to the Second Division, but also an era in the history of Swansea City. This was the final match played with Doug Sharpe as chairman, who had found another buyer and stood down, after a total period of some 14 years.

Doug's first substantive period in the chair had ended with the financial meltdown of 1985 but few fans blamed him for that situation. However, there is no doubt that Doug set the agenda that the revived club was to follow for the following decade. By the end many fans were glad to see the back of the chairman who had come in for increasing vilification. How will posterity view his record?

On the positive side, it should never be underestimated that Doug Sharpe did put his money where his mouth was and presented a package that kept the club alive. If he hadn't, Swansea City may have gone the way of Aldershot or Newport County. He also made a positive start to the new era by appointing Terry Yorath as manager and sanctioning the signing of players that won promotion at the second attempt. Both Yorath and Jan Molby attest to Doug's enthusiasm for the club in their autobiographies. The club initially consolidated its status in the old third division, and apparently operated on an even financial keel. Certainly the club never suffered the very threats to its existence during Doug's second spell in the chair that had occurred immediately before and were to threaten the club in the future. There was also a trophy won at Wembley while Frank Burrows built a team that was close to being genuine promotion contenders. A few years later the Sharpe period could be seen as a golden era of stability in relative terms. Why then did so many people feel relieved when Doug Sharpe finally walked away?

Perhaps the word that sums up supporter feeling of the later Sharpe years is frustration. How much of this had its roots in inflated expectations of the teams stature – particularly in the shadow of the Toshack era – will always be a matter of conjecture. However, as the years went by there was an increasing perception amongst supporters that the club was stagnating. The club never appeared able to build on promising situations as first Yorath and later Burrows pieced together teams of potential that was never to be realised. While there were occasional exhibitions of greater ambition in the transfer market, the perception was that the club had reverted to its stance a generation earlier of being primarily a selling club.

Allied to the frustrations on the pitch was a growing feeling in some quarters of the club becoming run down off it. The Vetch was looking increasingly shabby and truncated in an era when smart new stands and stadiums were springing up elsewhere. The club shop was looking dated at a time when most clubs were revolutionising their merchandising operations. The Swans increasingly resembled a small corner shop attempting to compete in the age of the shopping mall. While Doug did submit various proposals to the Council with a view to improving the ground situation, he never succeeded in persuading the powers that be of the merits of his schemes.

Yet even the stasis of the early 1990s was preferable to the depressing farce of the 1995-96 season when an under-strength team was relegated against a background of off-field chaos and managerial instability. Counsel for Sharpe's defence would probably have argued that the realities of the changes in British football finance were now starting to bite, and that in any event, there was substantial mitigation in the way that the Thompson sale was aborted and Molby appointed. However, to most supporters the truly frustrating thing was that the club had received a substantial transfer income of which only a relatively small part was re-invested on the pitch. Few expected wild expenditure, but the events of the season increased disillusion even amongst the hard core.

By the later days of the Sharpe regime the club were caught in a vicious circle. The club blamed the sale of players and failure to strengthen on poor support, but this in turn led to poor performances on the pitch that caused gates to decline even further. The public were voting with their feet as attendances began to slump to levels reminiscent of the mid 1970s. While the appointment of Molby stemmed the flow, the overall trend was not encouraging. Meanwhile the flow of financial information from the club had slowed to a trickle as the old annual meetings had been discontinued. Almost inevitably in such circumstances, gossip and innuendo spread through the support, and discontent with the Sharpe regime grew.

The lack of financial transparency was compounded by the employment of Doug's son Robin as Chief Executive, an easily foreseeable public relations disaster. Yet both criticisms belied a more fundamental difficulty not only with the Sharpe regime, but with the manner in which many British football clubs were traditionally run. Clubs were in the main private companies with only a limited obligation to make their internal affairs public. Concepts such as openness, transparency and accountability to the wider supporter body were not inherent to this model. Whilst legally this may have been justifiable, what this model failed to take into account was that spiritual ownership of the club extended well beyond the confines of the boardroom, and that supporters were emotional stakeholders. In this sense Doug Sharpe was in all probability no better or worse than dozens of old style club chairmen.

Yet by the late 1990s the classic model of the local businessman who doubled as football club chairman was about to change. Increasingly, club ownership was becoming the preserve of multi-millionaires and publicly quoted companies, as the business world's view of football changed. It was hardly Doug's personal fault that football was increasingly embarking on a course of financial madness that was to later have grave consequences for many a club. Many would say that Doug was right not to join the jamboree and spend in excess of the club's means. Nor was it his fault that he didn't have the personal fortune to compete with football's new money men. It was one thing for some elements on the North Bank to demand that Doug stand aside and make way for a person with greater resources to take over. History was to show that finding such a benefactor was to prove rather more difficult.

Doug Sharpe will be remembered for saving the club of which he was undoubtedly a fan. However, he will also be associated with a period of frustration when the club appeared to stand still and revert to its historic policy of selling its best young players. Yet perhaps he should be seen in the context of a style of club ownership that was not untypical in British football, but was now under challenge from differing directions. On the one hand the concept of a football club as a profit making business was changing. On the other, many supporters across Britain were seeking a greater say in the running of club affairs. Perhaps change was inevitable at this point. However, those who had been critical of Doug Sharpe's style and thought that things could not get any worse were in for a shock. The idea that closure of the Sharpe era was to spell an end to the club's problems was to prove well wide of the mark.

Wembley here we come! Carl Heggs scoring the third goal against Chester City at
The Vetch – play off semi-final second leg May 1997
(Photo: *South Wales Evening Post*)

Swansea City versus Northampton Town
Football League play-off final at Wembley, May 1997
(Photo: *South Wales Evening Post*)

Part three: Corporate men and chancers

8. Corked White

The events of May 1997 had seemed pivotal in the history of both Swansea City and Britain as a whole. Early that month a bright spring morning had seemed to herald a new dawn as a new regime in Westminster offered hope of change after several years of an administration that had become unpopular amidst allegations of incompetence and corruption. Later that same month Swansea supporters travelled to London on a similar sunny morning buoyed not only by the prospect of possible promotion, but also by the announcement that another regime that had grown unpopular was about to be replaced.

In both cases the hope was short lived and within months both the new Labour government and the new owners at the Vetch were attracting criticism. In both instances events evolved to result in widespread discontent and ultimately demonstration marches aimed at men named Tony. If the new dawn for Britain had led to disillusion in some quarters, the fresh start for the Swans was to ultimately lead to the near extinction of the club.

It was ironic that in waving goodbye to a man whose oft-repeated mantra was that he secured the existence of the club, we were to set off on a road that was to lead once again toward oblivion. After all, back in the summer of 1997, many fans felt genuinely optimistic. Swansea City were to be part of a new phenomenon that was sweeping through football, the profit seeking public limited company. The new owners were to be Silver Screen Windshields, a successful auto-windscreen company that were seeking to move into football club ownership. Abandoning their former trade, the company were to eventually assume the guise of Ninth Floor Limited.

The mechanics of the change of ownership seemed to drag on as the summer weeks went by, and with it seemed to pass the chance of strengthening the team. The story behind the delays varied with the teller. As far as supporters were concerned the only certainty was uncertainty, and several players remained out of contract as the new season approached. It seemed that until the change of ownership was completed these issues could not be resolved, while the club was also subject to a transfer embargo as a result of an outstanding Football League ground improvement loan.

It was difficult to believe that Jan Molby was happy as Dave Penney took up an offer from Cardiff, thus losing an experienced midfielder. Roger Freestone and Keith Walker remained in limbo for some weeks. In the meantime Carl Heggs left for Northampton while Dai Thomas was sold to Watford for £100,000. Even as the new season was upon the club and the new owners finally in place, Steve Torpey left for Bristol City for £400,000. If fans were divided on both Torpey and Thomas's merits, the loss of the previous season's entire strike force was hardly encouraging.

The optimists still hoped that the substantial fee received for Torpey would be made available to Molby. However, the main inward movements were Barry Town pair Tony Bird and Dave O'Gorman. Both had been important members of Barry's dominant League of Wales side, and both had impressed in the previous season's UEFA Cup run. Bird in particular had shown some promise as a youngster at Cardiff, and had revived his career by scoring prolifically in the League of Wales making his signing a worthwhile gamble. O'Gorman was a skilful forward who could operate in a variety of roles, but Molby may have had it in mind that he might be a more consistent creative force than the unpredictable Appleby. Neither, however, was a target man in the manner of Torpey, and it was to take the club some time to remedy that particular deficiency. The other recruit was Gary Jones, who had also been playing in the League of Wales with Caernarfon Town.

Despite three straight home wins, early form was disappointing, and cracks were showing in defence where the steadiness of Steve Jones was being missed. With Molby only appearing intermittently the team appeared to lack experience in too many areas, and while Jason Price, Jonathan Coates and Christian Edwards maintained their promise, it was clear that the team needed an injection of experience. In a torrid period for Welsh football, Bobby Gould's national team had lost 6-4 in Turkey as a result of some farcical defending. A few days later at Hull the Swans proved that they could go one better as the home side won 7-4. If that result increased the pressure on Molby, then a home defeat by Barry in the FAW Premier Cup and an away loss to Peterborough in the league gave the new board the chance that some fans subsequently believed they had sought from the outset. Molby was sacked as manager on the Monday after his inexperienced team lost at London Road.

Strangely, just days before his sacking, Molby was allowed to spend the considerable sum of just over £100,000 on Wrexham's Steve Watkin. To allow a manager whose neck was on the block to spend by the club's standards a large amount of money seemed decidedly confused. Ironically, Watkin proved to be one of Molby's better value for money signings. However, he was not the tall target man the side appeared to need, and while he was able to hold the ball up effectively, it was difficult to see a front line of Watkin and Bird having the physical presence to unnerve Third Division defences.

If the sequence of signing Watkin and then sacking Molby betrayed confusion in the boardroom, we hadn't seen anything yet. On the face of it the club made a sound appointment in Micky Adams, who had won promotion for Fulham the previous season and was unlucky to fall victim to Mohammed al Fayed's desire to appoint the higher profile Kevin Keegan. His recent success was encouraging, and the rumour mill suggested that Adams may have been the new owners' preferred choice even before the season began. If that was indeed the case then the events of the next fortnight became even more bizarre. Once again the

82

club attracted media attention of the wrong kind as Adams resigned after a mere 13 days. While not quite of the same order as the appointment of Kevin Cullis, the whole affair left a series of question marks hanging over the new board, and the feeling grew that the club had exchanged an old fashioned oligarch for shiny new corporatism to little practical effect.

Adams quit after three defeats, and the only certain thing appeared to be that the fans were not told the whole truth by either side. Adams maintained an outward claim of stolid professionalism, stating no direct reason for his sudden about turn, yet slightly detracted from this stance by alluding to having suffered similar problems to Jan Molby. Certainly this struck a chord with fans who were now disillusioned with the new regime within weeks of the takeover. There seemed little rhyme or reason to events and supporters were left wondering precisely what was going on behind the scenes.

Whatever the truth behind the public statements, the club was once again at the centre of managerial instability. The board appointed Adams' assistant Alan Cork as his successor, which meant that the club was in the hands of a novice manager for the second time in two years. Despite the new manager starting with two successive away wins, including a victory at Ninian Park thanks to a Keith Walker screamer, the team continued to struggle. Over three months went by without a win at home, a sequence that added to frustrations, as ironically away form was respectable if not spectacular. Aside from runaway leaders Notts County, and crisis club Doncaster, there seemed little between the remainder of the clubs in the division and a decent sequence of results could have won a play-off place. This said more about the mediocre nature of the league rather than anything positive about a stuttering Swans team that remained too close to the foot of the table for comfort.

Cork was given some leeway in the transfer market and, in fairness to him, and chief scout Ian Branfoot, made a series of shrewd signings. Nick Cusack, Matthew Bound and Julian Alsop all arrived over the course of the season to provide the spine of the side with a combination of experience and physical presence, while Michael Howard was to become a fixture at left back for seasons to come. Less successful was Aidan Newhouse, a striker who might politely be described as lacking mobility, while Charlie Hartfield never recovered from a poor start in midfield. At least the team now possessed a better balance of youth and experience.

The season's nadir was probably reached in a 2-0 home defeat by Barnet at Christmas, particularly as the second goal was one of the more farcical seen at the Vetch in recent seasons, the North Londoners scoring into an empty net with Roger Freestone up-field for a last minute corner. However, back-to-back wins in January over fellow strugglers Brighton and Hull brought the Swans back in touch with the mid-table pack and a period of better form followed over the next six weeks or so. In any event, Doncaster were stranded at the bottom in the midst of a dreadful off-field crisis, and the spectre of relegation to the Conference gradually receded as the green shoots of spring appeared.

The new signings added some solidity to the team, and with Tony Bird contributing 14 league goals there was some hope of a brighter future. Indeed, some felt that Bird would have scored more if he had been paired with a proper target man from the outset, although others pointed out that he scored more frequently in the early part of the season under Molby's passing style of football. In addition, Jonathan Coates scored eight and enjoyed what some people believe was his best season. Certainly his goal at Leyton Orient in February, a piledriver from 30 yards after a run from inside his own half, would have been a contender for Goal of the Month if scored in a higher division.

If Coates was to later become a frustrating player unable to produce what he was capable of on a regular basis, that role was already being performed by the enigmatic Richie Appleby. On his day probably the most gifted player in the squad, Appleby also appeared at times the most brainless, managing to get himself sent off on three occasions around the turn of the year. There was a feeling that literally anything could happen when he took the field. Occasionally this included football.

Off the pitch the new owners attempted to claw back some credibility with fans by unveiling plans for a new 25,000 seat stadium development at Morfa. Whilst all interested parties made the right noises, the Council did add the caveat that the development had to be right for all the citizens of Swansea. While planning consent seemed available in principle, the scheme was subject to the board finding the financial backing. The artists' impressions were typically impressive, but at this stage fans were far from convinced, having heard similar plans in the past that had failed to materialise. Until there were cranes over Morfa, few people would believe it was actually going to happen. The stadium saga was becoming part of the folklore of the club, and the bold plans did little to allay the pervasive sense of having been here before.

Meanwhile, former hero Robbie James collapsed and died on the pitch at a Welsh League match at Llanelli's Stebonheath Park, while appearing as player-manager for the home side. For anybody to die at the age of 40 seemed sad, but for Swans' fans of a certain age, the loss of a man who was synonymous with the success of the Toshack era was particularly poignant. Television eulogies featuring replays of his surging runs and devastating shooting reminded fans of what had been achieved nearly 20 years before, and how far the club had regressed since. Ivor Allchurch had died just before the season had commenced, and in just a few months the club had lost two of it's greatest ever players. The memories these two icons evoked seemed a long way from the rather grim reality of life in the Third Division in the late 1990s.

The season had been largely a non-event on the pitch for Swansea City, and while the club never descended into a true playing crisis, there was little to suggest a revival was imminent. Three successive away defeats at the season's end contributed to a 20th place finish, the worst since the dog days of the 1974-75 re-election team. Indeed, this could be argued to be worse, for at least in those days the likes of Alan Curtis and Robbie James provided a genuine glimmer of hope for the future. To provide a depressing parallel, crowds had dipped and there were also concerns about the team's disciplinary record. Those of a parochial state of mind drew comfort from finishing one place above Cardiff City, a shabby 'achievement' that reflected poorly on Welsh football as a whole.

Swansea supporters could see the club going one of two ways over the summer of 1998. Hopefully the club could re-group in the manner of Harry Griffiths's side in the mid-1970s. Alternatively the writing was on the wall for another season of struggle. At that point the new bosses had shown little to prove that they were any different to the old boss. Swans' fans were not in the mood to be fooled again.

*   *   *

Just when it seemed there was a little stability in the manager's office, those who ran Swansea City decided that life was getting a little boring and that things needed livening up. The result was a further period of disruption with inevitable consequences on the pitch. The ghost of managerial farces past began to haunt supporters as the Swans' record of hiring and firing began to rival that of Atletico Madrid's infamous President Jesus Gil. Gil once famously sacked Ron Atkinson after a mere 56 days in the job. Big Ron never applied for a job at Swansea, presumably reasoning that he didn't want to face the potential embarrassment of beating his own record. After all, 56 days seemed like a job for life compared to the reigns of Kevin Cullis and Micky Adams.

What then of the three incumbents of Swansea City's latest managerial merry-go-round? The most mourned was undoubtedly Jan Molby. Yet looked at in the cold light of day the Dane's overall league record was far from spectacular. The club were relegated from a difficult but not irretrievable position in his first season, while the prosecution would also point to his transfer record, including money spent to little effect on the likes of Moreira, Brown and Garnett. At the time of his sacking the Swans were positioned dangerously near the foot of the table.

All of this is true, yet the negative aspects of Molby's period in charge are mitigated by a number of factors. Firstly, he arrived as a manager with no experience at a club that were in complete chaos, restored a little pride and at least initially led a minor revival. The playing squad had been weakened well before he arrived, and he did at least correctly identify the areas of the team that needed strengthening, even if his choice of personnel was to prove disappointing. Perhaps a more experienced manager might have made better choices, but in truth, this only begs the question as to whether he was the right choice for the situation the club found itself in, and whether he should have been given experienced assistance from the outset.

85

Indeed, the early signs of Molby's first full season in charge were not encouraging, and had things not improved by Christmas the Sharpe axe might well have fallen. However, something clicked with the team, and the middle of the 1996-97 season was one of the brighter periods in the recent history of the club, in terms not only of results, but of the football the team were attempting to play.

One can only speculate as to how differently things might have worked out if luck had been on their side at Wembley. As it was, Molby's efforts to go one better the following season were undermined by off the field events and the loss of key players to other clubs. There was certainly a perception amongst supporters that Molby had not been given a fair crack of the whip by the new owners. Had he been allowed to spend money in the close season and the team had started badly, one would have sensed the board's frustrations. That he was sacked having been denied that luxury fuelled the conspiracy theories.

Certainly Molby did not appear to enjoy a good working relationship with Steve Hamer. Whilst the chairman's frustration at not seeing Molby take the field more often was understandable, it was surely the case that a player of his ability was only at Swansea in the first place because of fitness problems during his final years at Liverpool. While there may have been issues as to Molby's level of conditioning, they were hardly novel, as he had never been the most svelte of players. Rather as in the case of John Toshack, perhaps it may have been unrealistic to expect a regular playing contribution.

Whatever the truth behind the scenes, Molby emerged as one of the more popular recent Swansea managers, despite his modest success rate. His subsequent record at Kidderminster showed that he was capable of building an effective team on a limited budget, although a subsequent spell at Hull and return to Kidderminster proved less successful. However, Molby was probably popular because he sat well with the perceptions of the club amongst its fan-base. Whether this was a case of celtic self delusion or not, the Swansea public like to see a team that not only wins, but also wins in an entertaining style. Molby's philosophy of football, honed in the neat passing schools of Ajax and Liverpool, sat well with a club that saw itself as embodying the spirit of Ivor Allchurch.

Bearing this in mind, it would have been interesting to see what the crowd would have made of Micky Adams had he stayed. It is unfair to pass any judgement on Adams' three games in charge, but what is undeniable is that he has gone on to confirm his reputation as one of the brighter young managers in the game, winning promotion for both Brighton and Leicester amidst difficult financial circumstances. His leaving was shrouded in mystery, but one can readily appreciate why the board felt he was the man to take the club forward. There is certainly reason to believe that if he had stayed rather longer that Adams could have moulded an effective Swansea team.

Yet in some ways, the word 'effective' damns Adams with faint praise, and is suggestive of potential for discontent on the Vetch Field terraces and stands. His Fulham side were not renowned for pretty football, and he has tended to be associated with a high tempo energetic style where athleticism is valued more than aestheticism. His right hand men, Alan Cork and Ian Branfoot were unequivocally associated with the long ball game. Branfoot, in particular had been forced out of the manager's job at Southampton by fan discontent due to his direct style of play. Would the Swansea public forgive the abandonment of the beautiful game if a more pragmatic approach brought results? Certainly this was a gamble on the new board's part, for Hamer as a local man should surely have appreciated that a more direct style was likely to result in restlessness on the terraces, particularly if the ends didn't justify the means.

Similar problems were always likely to make Alan Cork's reign difficult. In many ways, Cork was on a hiding to nothing, effectively perceived as Molby's replacement, and at all times moving in his shadow. Molby had come across in the media as a charismatic and articulate, while Cork appeared pleasant but slightly uncertain. Adams may have had the confidence and lucidity win over the doubters and make a change of playing style work, but Cork seemed to be fighting an uphill battle from the outset.

Rightly or wrongly, Swansea City fans have a perception of the club as embodying the positive virtues of skilled attacking football. Rather like the fans of West Ham or Tottenham, Swansea fans believed in certain values of passing, control and skill. Jan Molby sat comfortably with that rather rose tinted image, whereas Alan Cork did not. Whilst he may have been stereotyped from the outset, Cork's inevitable association with Wimbledon and their image of bar-room brawls brought onto the field did not appeal to the Swansea fan base.

Yet for all the reservations that the crowd may have fairly or otherwise held regarding the style of play under Alan Cork, one suspects that ultimately he was undone by results. Whatever the circumstances, 20th place was not a good finish, particularly in such an average division. After all, the previous season, Molby's team had reached the play-offs from a similar position in October to the one that Cork inherited. The feeling was that Cork had only landed the job by default when Adams left, and the board wanted to avoid even more instability. It always seemed likely that the club would go back to the drawing board come the season's end unless he had exceeded all expectations. Yet it should also be said that Cork's dealings in the transfer market set in place the foundations of a team that was to achieve success in the future, and represented good value for money.

Meanwhile, Swansea fans were becoming accustomed to perpetual revolution in the manager's office. Stability was to arrive, but not before further change. When it did arrive, many fans questioned the credentials of the incumbent. That was for the future. In the short term it seemed things could only get better, and for a while it seemed they did.

As Swansea City's season ended with a whimper and the players went on holiday, another match was taking place at Wembley that was to prove significant in its own way. The game, while spectacular in itself, was a staging post on the route to success for a club who were to confound the views of those who believed that progress to the highest level could now only be achieved through recklessly waving a cheque book.

The First Division play-off Final between Charlton Athletic and Sunderland proved to be one of the most exciting matches ever staged at the old stadium. Charlton's success on penalties after extra time had seen the sides locked at 4-4 represented one of the more heart-warming stories of British football in the late 20th century. Charlton's progress was an example for all medium-sized clubs across the country, and when set against the background of the club's struggle to return to its traditional home was truly remarkable. That this was not achieved through some fairy godfather millionaire exercising his ego, but through a genuine collective effort of fans and board working together, ought to be an inspiration to any club of a similar size.

For those who are unaware of the tale, it is one worth recounting. Charlton's problems had come to a head in September 1985 when the club were forced to leave The Valley and become tenants at Selhurst Park. At that stage, the club were looking all set for a slow death. However, the club's fans seized the moment, and the 'Back to The Valley' campaign gradually gathered momentum. Local Council opposition to their return was countered by fans forming their own single-issue political party to contest local elections. The individual talents and contacts of supporters were exploited to the full.

In December 1992 Charlton returned to their traditional home amidst a huge wave of local emotion. However, behind the euphoria of the return, the reality was threadbare. The ground was three-sided, one of which consisted of a temporary scaffolding stand and temporary dressing rooms. The great East Terrace lay cracked and derelict, openly mocking the ambitions of those who had built the Football League's largest ground, a backdrop to years of underachievement and financial mismanagement. On the pitch the team were struggling under the management of the recently appointed rookie, Alan Curbishley. Capacity at the time was a mere 8,000, but this didn't look as if it would be tested on a regular basis. The entire operation was as ramshackle as the ground.

The reality for Charlton was that despite the apparent victory of their return to their home ground, the club was in financial dire straits, and the return home was the first staging post in a larger struggle, not success in itself. What Charlton used to their advantage was that the battle for the Valley had brought together the board and supporters in a special way. The board didn't consist of hopeful speculators, but of men who were Charlton to the core. The supporters didn't sit about whingeing, but actively became involved in both the return to the old ground and the rebuilding of the club. The supporters were rewarded with one of the first

88

genuine 'fan on the board' schemes. Both board and fans were rewarded with mutual respect and trust.

Growth was gradual, as supporters acknowledged that the survival of the club was paramount, even if that meant a lowering of sights in the short term. For the first few seasons, results were somewhat mediocre. Where success was obvious, however, was in the gradual growth of support through schemes such as 'Target Ten Thousand'. Charlton reached out energetically into the schools, youth groups and other community organisations, trying to turn around the 40 years of neglect that had seen a leakage of support to more fashionable clubs. Efforts were made to eradicate a small pocket of racist support to encourage the belief that The Valley was a safe environment to visit. The club didn't spend money they didn't have, but built a team over a period of years.

Even in the aftermath of the Wembley success, there was no giving in to the temptation to spend money that would mortgage the club's future, but instead a gradual strengthening of the squad and expansion of the ground. That has placed the club in a position of genuine playing and financial strength. Initial relegation was not the crisis it became at other clubs and the club bounced back at the first attempt. Past lessons of financial mismanagement were taken on board and the quick fix eschewed in favour of sustainable development. Today, the club are well established in the Premiership, and their traditional home has been developed into a state of the art stadium. Look at the playing fields of South East London today and the Charlton replica kits outnumber the ubiquitous Manchester United and Liverpool.

At the time of Charlton's Wembley glory, Swansea fans might have looked at the manner in which the South East London club was run with a certain wistfulness. Not only was it successful on the pitch, but it was run by a board who seemed to combine good husbandry and commercial acumen with a fan friendly approach. This contrasted with successive administrations at the Vetch who could have taken lessons from their counterparts at the Valley in terms of public relations.

Yet Charlton was also to show a way forward a few years later when Swansea fans were to face their own problems. As in South East London, supporters had to take matters into their own hands to save the club they loved. Charlton had shown what could be achieved when supporters from all walks of life pulled together in the same direction. For those who believed that a football club was about more than egotistical entrepreneurs and profit margins, and that clubs could be run with the genuine interests of supporters and communities at heart, events at the Valley showed that the dream could become reality.

When Charlton claimed their place in the Premiership at Wembley in May 1998, it was not just a victory for one particular club, but an example for every small and medium sized club whose existence had been called into doubt, a victory for the soul of football and a benchmark for a club such as Swansea City.

Swansea City versus West Ham United, FA Cup replay, January 1999
(Photo: *South Wales Evening Post*)

Kristian O'Leary (Photo: Andrew Thomas)

The Championship decider:
Rotherham United versus Swansea City Division 3 May 2000
(Photo: *South Wales Evening Post*)

Celebrating the Championship win in May 2000
(Photo: *South Wales Evening Post*)

Roger Freestone – Swansea goalkeeping legend.
(Photo: *South Wales Evening Post*)

9.   Purple rain

It is fair to say that South West Wales is hardly a stranger to mist and rain. One would be hard pressed to think of a season that didn't feature at least one home fixture that wasn't washed away. However, the 1998-99 campaign seemed particularly extreme as a succession of home matches were either postponed or played against a watery backdrop on a pitch that resembled a paddy field. These were the days when it seemed to rain forever.

All of this seemed a long way off during the early summer. Transfer activity was relatively quiet, the main outward movement being Christian Edwards who left for the greener climes of Nottingham Forest. This was hardly a surprise, as rumours had abounded of the young defender's possible departure prior to the previous season's transfer deadline. It seemed Swans fans were becoming inured to the disappointment of seeing the club's best young prospects depart. One could hardly blame Edwards for wanting to play at a higher level of football, and few Jacks felt confident that he could achieve it at the Vetch in the immediate future. What put matters into perspective, however, was that Edwards was some way from walking straight into Forest's first team.

Other departures included Lynton Brown, although this was also of little surprise for quite different reasons. Brown appeared mercurial, occasionally capable of flashes of great skill, but more often of anonymity. Two other players were to play little part in the forthcoming season due to career ruining injury. If Charlie Hartfield was missed by few, the loss of Keith Walker was sad, as he had given the club years of good service.

Having lost two key defenders, Cork sought to cover the gap by signing Jason Smith from Tiverton Town. Smith was to prove an inspired signing and was about to embark on the two best seasons of his career. Cork's other signing renewed the Fulham connection when Martin Thomas arrived, having proved surplus to the al Fayed revolution. Both Smith and Thomas were to prove excellent signings, playing vital parts in the season's major success, and confirming Cork's apparent ability to play the transfer market well.

Not that Cork would be around to see how his new charges would fare. As June closed, so did the manager's tenure. If few Swans fans were either surprised or upset over his departure, the timing once again appeared odd. If Cork had been dismissed after the final game of the previous season, few would have demurred. However, to allow the manager to make new signings carried echoes of allowing Molby to sign Steve Watkin and then sacking him within days.

The rumour mill had it that the Swans were looking to appoint an experienced manager. In the event the new man was to be former Chelsea and QPR midfielder John Hollins, arguably better known for his role in anti-smoking campaigns than for club management. Hollins had experienced an ill-starred period in charge of Chelsea, and although few would blame him for failing to turn around that ailing giant at the time, his most recent job had been with QPR reserves. These hardly seemed the credentials of experience that the club allegedly sought. While prepared to give Hollins a chance, many fans were distinctly under-whelmed.

On the positive side, Hollins had been a neat and industrious midfielder with both Chelsea and QPR teams that won plaudits for their skilful attacking football in the 1970s. If fans had never truly accepted Cork, viewing him as a proponent of direct football, Hollins did at least retain associations with a passing game. If he didn't exactly set the town talking, fans seemed to want to put the Cork era behind them, and were there to be persuaded as to the new manager's worth.

Hollins got off to a winning start against Exeter at the Vetch, and there followed a further positive performance in a drawn League Cup tie against First Division Norwich. Perhaps the most memorable thing about that match, however, was the bizarre encounter between Norwich manager Bruce Rioch and new mascot Cyril the Swan. Rioch had not been one to shirk a challenge as a player, but to see him in an altercation with a nine foot tall fluffy bird was distinctly surreal.

If the Swans were unlucky to go out of that competition after taking the second leg into extra time, league form was not so encouraging. Rather like the previous two seasons, the team struggled in September and found themselves at the wrong end of the table. One point from five matches provided plenty for the pessimists to feed on and in the light of the previous season, even the most optimistic fans were nervous. Fortunately matters began to improve and the team began to pick up points, including a 3-1 win over Southend when the visitors had two men sent off, a feat that they were to better some years later. However, a failure to turn draws into wins meant that the club continued to languish in the lower half of the table, a performance that was all the more frustrating as Cardiff City made an early drive for promotion following the return of Frank Burrows as manager.

The FA Cup was to prove the turning point and exercised a huge influence on the season. Few gave much for the Swans' chances when they drew Second Division Millwall at home in the first round. Instead, defying the form book, the Swans produced their best performance of the season to demolish the Lions by 3-0. If Jason Price was expecting some positive headlines for an impressive performance, however, he was to hope in vain, as Cyril the Swan became the centre of attention after running onto the field to help celebrate a goal. Whether this diversion of media attention from the team onto the mascot with the burgeoning notorious reputation was a good thing was to become a debateable point.

Buoyed by this success, the Swans proceeded to kick start the hitherto somnambulant league season to life with an epic 2-1 victory over Cardiff at the Vetch. Outplayed in the first half, the Swans dug deep in the second, and goals from Martyn Thomas and Matthew Bound sealed victory. Frank Burrows had been warmly received by most Swans fans, and was both dignified and magnanimous in defeat. He could afford to be, as his side looked a good bet for promotion notwithstanding the result, while the Swans were going to have to go some to catch up.

Rather like two years earlier, the team embarked on its best run of league form of the season during November and December, winning five out of seven matches. The Swans moved into the upper part of mid table, well set for a promotion challenge in the New Year, although they were not to move into the play-off spots until the final week of the season, playing the shadiest of dark horses.

This was in part due to the weather, which caused the postponement of two home league fixtures, and partly the FA Cup, which further disrupted the fixture schedule. The second round had brought Second Division leaders Stoke to the Vetch, and again few believed that the Swans would come out on top despite the improved league form. While almost falling behind to what would have been a spectacular own goal when Jason Smith accidentally headed against his own crossbar, the Swans took the lead through Richie Appleby, and withstood a second half barrage to earn a place in the third round draw.

Appleby was proving to be his usual enigmatic self, combining the sublime with the frustrating. His mazy run past half the Rotherham team to set up an equaliser on a Friday night in October had been truly mesmerising. Unfortunately, equally typical was his sending off at Southend for a late challenge within minutes of coming on as a substitute. By the end of the season Appleby's role as the man most likely to turn a match had been usurped by a young player from Llanelli named Stuart Roberts, who was to make his name with two electric performances against West Ham in the third round of the FA Cup.

In the first match at Upton Park, Roberts run and cross set up a goal for Jason Smith to give the Swans the lead. The team played out of their skins, only to be denied by a late long-range effort from Julian Dicks that Roger Freestone appeared to see late through a forest of legs. Off the pitch, the Jack Army reminded West Ham of the level of noise that could be generated by fans, testimony to the decline in atmosphere at what had been one of the loudest grounds in the country before the inception of all-seating stadiums.

Most Swans' fans believed a golden opportunity for a giant killing had disappeared with Dicks' equaliser. With hindsight, the notoriously aggressive defender may have regretted scoring that goal, for without it he would have been spared the torment that effectively finished off his West Ham career. Stuart Roberts gave the left back a torrid evening in the replay, and Hammers' manager Harry Redknapp quickly moved to sign a replacement. If the Swansea crowd had needed gccing up any further, a series of challenges by Dicks and fellow hard man Neil Ruddock did the trick. Dicks the reputed fan of heavy metal music would have appreciated the loud and raucous noise emanating from the North Bank. Dicks the footballer would have wished he'd stayed at home. Cyril the Swan may have been on his way to a career in pantomime, but Dicks and Ruddock were not to be upstaged, the two cartoon-like ageing villains playing their traditional role to a deafening chorus of boos and jeers.

Roberts performance was matched by Martin Thomas who played arguably his best ever game in a Swansea shirt, scoring the winner, and coming close on at least two other occasions. Ruddock looked as if he might have the last laugh when he fiendishly struck a thunderbolt toward the corner of the Swans net with minutes remaining. Roger Freestone flung himself as if a genie propelled by a stage trap-door, and granted all our wishes by diverting the ball around the post to foil the dastardly villain and ensure that the good guys in white had won.

The match had provided a strange homecoming for West Ham's Welsh international striker John Hartson, a self acknowledged Swans' fan, who was occasionally seen watching the team he had grown up supporting when his professional schedule allowed. There was also a return to the Vetch for Frank Lampard, who had spent a successful loan spell at the Swans in 1995-96, and who was to go on to achieve rather better things in the coming years with both Chelsea and England.

If the Swans were home and dry in the third round, the fourth was to see them home and distinctly wet. Derby came to the Vetch in a West Wales winter squall, and hopes of a further upset were high. Whilst most of the pre-match media attention had been focussed on Cyril the Swan rather than the team, the match turned into something of an anti-climax. Despite the chauvinistic talk in some sections of the media about their 'fancy dan' foreign stars not having the stomach for a battle, Derby defended resolutely, restricting the Swans to half chances. Inevitably, one of the 'fancy dans', Argentine sweeper Carbonari, set up the late goal that won the match for Derby.

Perhaps more depressing than the weather or the result was the sight of publicity magnet Cyril the Swan having abandoned his Swans top in favour of a tee-shirt advertising *The Sun.* That some people would prefer 20 pieces of silver to the integrity of the club was tawdry enough, but for others the fact that the club was prepared to endorse a newspaper that had proved itself a poor friend to football supporters in the days after the Hillsborough disaster evidenced a lack of taste.

On a more positive note, whatever fans ultimately came to think of John Hollins, there was little doubt that he had presided over a series of results that had lifted spirits at the club, and that had created a massive buzz in the city. The atmosphere on the night of the West Ham match, and the general talk surrounding the club were arguably the most positive since the Toshack era. After all the negative publicity of the previous few years, the fans once again had something to cheer on the pitch.

Some supporters were a little relieved that the cup run was over, allowing the team to concentrate on a promotion push in the league.

While the Swans now had a number of games in hand on their rivals due to the various postponements, there was every danger of a massive fixture pile up come the season's end. Also those games had to be turned into points, something which was to prove difficult in practice. Whether the cup run had unduly distracted the players was a debateable point. Certainly the 4-0 defeat at Exeter sandwiched between the West Ham games was universally acknowledged as the worst performance of the season. What was undisputable was the cost in injuries as both Roger Freestone and Martin Thomas faced lengthy lay-offs as a result of knocks sustained in cup games.

A series of home draws and defeat at bottom club Scarborough meant the team progressed in fits and starts and the possibility of automatic promotion gradually disappeared. For those in love with the club, this team was a tease, always promising consummation, but leaving fulfilment tantalisingly a touch away. In some senses, the league season was encapsulated in the home match with Plymouth in April. Two up at half time the team proceeded to commit defensive suicide and lose 3-2. At that point many fans thought that the club had blown its chance, particularly as two of the final three games were against championship contenders Brentford and Cambridge. Enigmatic to the last, the team won three out of the last four to clinch a play-off spot. As if to emphasise the part that the weather had played in the season, the final home game against Hull was delayed by 40 minutes due to heavy morning rain that had left the Vetch pitch once again resembling a lake. This might have proved controversial, although in the event the rival teams all dropped points, making the Vetch result irrelevant. Two goals from Steve Watkin sealed the game, prompting the second mass celebration at the Vetch that season.

In the end the play-offs proved a game too far. Ironically, the fans felt a surge of confidence, and there were echoes of 1987-88 when a mediocre league season had ended in promotion via the play-offs with a late burst of form. Scunthorpe United stood between the Swans and a third trip to Wembley in six seasons. Certainly the Swans replicated 1988 by winning the home leg of the play-off semi-final by the only goal. Had a Tony Bird shot gone just inside the post instead of coming back off it the psychological impetus would have been firmly in the all white direction. Instead, in a highly charged atmosphere at Glanford Park, Brian Laws' team came out kicking and fighting, and the Swans' lead was soon cancelled out. The game went into extra time and despite a Bird goal giving hope, the Swans lost 3-2 on aggregate to a side that might euphemistically have been described as 'competitive'. There were certainly those in the Swansea camp who felt that a stronger referee might have been less permissive. As it was, the season was over – another play-off, another disappointment.

Yet the season had been far from disastrous. Certainly the seventh place finish represented a substantial improvement in league position compared to a year before, while the FA Cup run had promoted a feel good factor. Steve Watkin had enjoyed a good season, his 17 league goals a good return for a player not necessarily seen as a prolific scorer. In this regard Tony Bird had been disappointing, failing to build on his promising goal return of the previous season. More positively, young players such as Jason Price and Stuart Roberts had emerged as genuinely creative forces, although goals never seemed easy to come by.

Indeed, one of the concerns for some supporters was that the further the season progressed, the more direct the team's football seemed to become. At the season's outset it had seemed that Hollins had encouraged a passing game. However, the inconsistent spring had seen a number of performances that saw a more direct approach. Possibly Hollins had decided that form was so inconsistent that a more pragmatic approach was needed. However, it was also true that by the time the second half of the season came around the Vetch pitch was in an awful state, full of bumps and bare patches. Perhaps there was a degree of pay-back, because one of the factors that had upset West Ham now seemed to be working in favour of the likes of Carlisle. Certainly it did not encourage passing football. Whether it was due to a developing street-wiseness or the effect of all that rain, pragmatism was to play a rather larger part in life over the next 12 months than most Swans fans had been accustomed to.

*   *   *

The close season of 1998 had seen the club once again unveil new home and away kits. The new home shirt was arguably the classiest for some years, being essentially an all white design, featuring minimal trimmings and the club's brand new badge. At first glance this should have had the purists purring, as the simplicity of the design was a relief after the squiggles, stripes and other excesses of the mid-1990s. The kit design was testimony to the concept of less being more, and suggested a modern version of the classic shirts of the Toshack era. However, closer examination would have also made the traditionalist seethe, as it became apparent that the trimmings were purple, causing many fans to groan. What was wrong with the old white and black?

The motivation behind this experiment seems to have been a desire to feature the corporate colour scheme of the City and County of Swansea in the club kit. Certainly the rugby club, who were to share the proposed Morfa development, had made a similar move by adding a series of maroon bars to their traditionally white shirts. Not that the sought-after cosiness with the Council lasted for long. The local authority seemed less than impressed with certain aspects of Ninth Floor's plans for the new stadium and relations between the club and Council soon became strained. After two seasons the purple phase was abandoned, but instead of having regard to the wishes of supporters which a reasoned bystander might have thought would have benefited potential sales, there was to be no return to black and white. Instead the red of Wales was to find its way into the home kit, via a broad stripe below the sleeves. Throughout these sartorial innovations, many fans were wondering why a classically simple white shirt with black trim could not be produced.

Yet attempts to meddle with what most fans considered the club's traditional home colours were not without precedent. Back in the early 1960s the black trim had been abandoned for orange, possibly in some quaint attempt to make the team look more Swan-like. Those were after all more innocent times, when clubs openly attempted to encourage cosy images based on nicknames such as the Pensioners and the Glaziers. While the idea of the Chelsea ear-trumpet and Crystal Palace putty-kit filling the shelves of their respective club superstores has its charm, somehow you can't see modern marketing gurus going for it. Whatever the aesthetic merits of Swansea's experiment in ornithological imitation, the team wore the kit successfully in the run to the 1964 FA Cup semi-final. Had the team won through to Wembley, might white and orange have become established as the club colours?

Certainly, there were many precedents for clubs giving themselves a makeover in terms of colour scheme, most famously at Leeds where manager Don Revie abandoned the yellow and blue stripes of the John Charles era in favour of the Real Madrid look sported to this day. A few years later Malcolm Allison changed Crystal Palace's colours, badge and nickname. Indeed the 1970s saw a number of attempts to paint over the cracks of many creaking clubs with a set of nice new colours, including Newport County's incongruous flirtation with going Argentine.

At the Vetch, Harry Gregg was not to be outdone. The Swans had abandoned the orange and reverted to white and black by the late 1960s, but Gregg saw the opportunity to become football's early version of Lawrence Llewellyn-Bowen, and give the club a complete makeover. White and black became white and red, while a dragon adorned the shirts in place of a swan. Presumably this was all in an effort to both accentuate the club's Welsh identity and also appear more modern and aggressive. While the disciplinary record of the Gregg era suggested that we possessed a number of players who could spit fire in the manner of strange and untamed animals, results were rather more consistent with the dragons having regularly run into St George. Meanwhile, the fans became confused as to what colours they should be sporting. The change didn't last long and before the Toshack era the team were back in white and black

By the 1990s the manufacture and sale of replica kits had become big business and one of the more contentious aspects of the football boom. While replica kits had been available for many years, the market had been limited for many years. In the 1970s and 1980s it had been so unsafe to wear colours at most grounds, particularly away from home, that few supporters openly displayed their allegiance unless they actively courted trouble. By the mid-1990s, however, the peaceable fan was in a more confident frame of mind, and the streets around most Premiership grounds were filled with both home and away spectators openly wearing club shirts. Most famously, the Newcastle bar-code army turned St James Park into a giant zebra crossing.

While the ability of fans to wear colours openly could be argued to be a positive development, the flip side of the coin was financial. Despite costing an apparent pittance to produce, the ordinary fan had to pay up to £40 for a replica shirt sporting club colours, or in some cases, what the latest club colours were deemed to be. Many of the results of designer's deliberations were garish, and often appeared to ignore clubs' traditions.

The Swans were hardly immune to this phenomenon. In 1992 the Swans trotted out in a kit covered with strange squiggles that in the opinion of more than one Swans supporter suggested that it had been originated while the designer was on a train that had gone over a set of points at speed. There also appeared a red wave amongst the black and white, a move that was here to stay in the short term, as red flashes turned up in both the bars and stripes design of the Autoglass Final kit, and the pinstripe 'sensible pyjamas' ensemble of 1995. A personal thought was that the latter resembled something that somebody's granny might have chosen for them for Christmas, although whether this was a deliberate ploy to boost sales was hard to say.

If the home kits of the period had traditionalists tearing their hair out, the away kit introduced in 1993 took matters to new extremes. The club's shirt sponsor at the time was Gulf Oil, and one can only assume the fluorescent orange and blue creation was intended to make the players resemble petrol pumps. Those who remember Chris Burns, who made a number of appearances during that period, would probably find it deeply ironic that the midfield player was being used as an advertisement for any product that wished to be associated with speed and motion.

It is of course, true that kit design is very much a matter of personal taste and that one man's meat is another's poison. Yet a succession of regimes at the club appeared to ignore a very straightforward answer to the question of kit design that has worked well with other clubs. A limited number of professionally produced designs could be put to the fans, and a vote taken for the preferred one. This has the advantage of fulfilling both supporter democracy and market research in one fell swoop.

The net effect of all the chopping and changing of trim was to make the Swans' end in high profile matches a confusion of colour-schemes. Study pictures of the Swansea end in the Toshack era – Plymouth, Preston and Liverpool being three examples - and one sees a sea of black and white. Fast forward to the end of the millennium and we see a varied mix of white with black, purple and red. Throw in a few away tops and we truly were the Technicolor dream-coat army.

When Silver Shield took over the club there was hope that they would improve the Swans' commercial operations including the shop, merchandising and other public interfaces. There were certainly financial incentives to do so. However, by the time Ninth Floor disposed of its interest in the club, it was questionable as to how much had fundamentally changed. Across the country clubs of all sizes were exploiting the merchandising opportunities of the football boom. A club didn't need to be Manchester United to cash in, as was proved by the likes of Charlton, who ran a well stocked shop even in the days when they commanded average gates of well under 10,000. Size didn't necessarily reflect on efficiency. The Swans shop meantime resembled a throwback to another era, as aside from a new but limited range of products in the ever-evolving club colours, little fundamental change was apparent.

The one major development on the marketing front was the appearance of Cyril the Swan, who first appeared by absailing into the Vetch in the summer of 1998. His place in the mascot hall of fame was guaranteed when the Welsh FA fined the club £1000 after Cyril had run onto the pitch to celebrate a goal. While the Welsh FA were derided in many quarters for their stance – particularly as their response to issues of violence and racism was rather less energetic – the cynical couldn't help thinking that the entire affair had done Cyril's sponsors no harm. There was little fundamentally wrong with the concept of a mascot, and there was much to be said for ensuring that the mascot was not as anodyne as at some clubs. However, there seemed to be points in the season when Cyril commanded more attention than events on the pitch, and some fans began to wonder whether the cart wasn't so much coming before the horse as being actively driven by it.

Even accepting Cyril at face value as a bit of good natured knock-about humour, there was something distinctly tiresome about the constant media attention given to the big bird during the 1998-99 FA Cup run. While Cyril generated some publicity, most fans would have preferred it if attention was focused the achievements of the team. Instead, at times it seemed as if the FA Cup run was merely a device to develop Cyril's media career. Before the Derby match it was impossible to get away from this pantomime persona, and one wonders what the team truly thought about this behind the public smiles. Whilst some people thought BBC pundit Mark Lawrenson was being unduly po-faced when he caustically commented that it didn't say much for Swansea as a city if Cyril the Swan was personality of the year, there were others who thought he might have a point.

Whilst there was an argument that Cyril was attractive to children, and helped draw a younger audience to the Vetch, the counter was that ultimately only a team that was worth watching would attract a long-term audience. The club's core business was after all supposed to be football rather than puppetry. In the meantime the changes of club colours were the subject of discontent amongst many supporters. If the board were serious about revolutionising the merchandising aspects of the club, they seemed to be ignoring the wishes of the club's fans.

If the manner of the play–off semi-final defeat at Scunthorpe left a nasty taste in the mouth, frustration was heightened by Cardiff City's escape from the Third Division through automatic promotion. That the success had been engineered by Frank Burrows, who many Swans' fans felt would have still been doing a good job at the Vetch had he been given support at boardroom level, rubbed salt into the wound. The subsequent histories of the clubs mean that they have not since met in a league fixture.

The Swans' relationship with their closest geographical rivals has grown increasingly fractious and volatile as the years have gone by. The two cities have always enjoyed a certain amount of commercial and sporting rivalry, being the largest conurbations in the old South Wales industrial belt. However, until more recent times there was little evidence that this had got out of hand. Indeed, the supporters of both teams applauded the other's successes during the growth years of South Wales professional football between the wars. It seemed a sense of 'Welshness' outweighed local one-upmanship. There was much co-operation between the professional clubs of the area in the period, particularly in the dealings with the administrators of English football and Welsh rugby.

While Cardiff City could justifiably claim to have enjoyed the better historical playing record, overall this was far from illustrious, while the Swans would claim to have been a more prodigious breeding ground of talent. Tellingly, much of both clubs' history had been played in the old Second Division. Whether the profile of rugby union in South Wales adversely affected the development of the football clubs is a moot point, but in practical terms, the area never became a football hotbed in the manner of other industrial areas, and the clubs never truly became iconic. Liverpool versus Manchester United or Newcastle versus Sunderland this was not.

However, the rivalry was ratcheted up a few notches in the late 1970s, and a certain John Benjamin Toshack was to play a pivotal role. As a young player, Toshack played in Cardiff City's last truly decent team, which narrowly missed out on promotion to the old First Division. He went on to live his dreams at Liverpool, but when he returned, it was not to his old stamping ground as anticipated by many at Ninian Park, but to place his name indelibly in the history of Swansea City. Suddenly the balance of power in Welsh club football lay at the western end of the M4, a shock to the natural order of things as perceived by many in the Welsh capital, who found the turnaround in fortunes difficult to stomach. That this revolution had been engineered by one of their own turned the knife a further twist. For years Cardiff City had been desperate for success, but had been unable to truly deliver. Now they could only look on in envy as Wales' second city left them behind. The pain for some Bluebird fans was just too much to bear.

As it turned out, the Swans' ascendancy was short lived. Both clubs had fallen upon hard times from the mid-1980s onwards, with lower division mediocrity largely the order of the day. Swansea City versus Cardiff City could not be classified as a great football occasion on the field. Yet had the rivalry between the clubs been limited to comparisons of on-field records and playing alumni, there would have been little to distinguish it from many other low key local derbies. Unfortunately, by the mid-1990s the fixture had assumed a reputation for spectator violence wholly disproportionate to its sporting worth.

While it is not the purpose of this book to analyse in detail the causes and rise of football violence, it was undoubtedly true to say that, in South Wales, it developed alongside the terminal industrial decline of the area. The presence of the Swans in the lower divisions in the late 1960s and early 1970s meant that the initial explosion largely passed Swansea by. There were few enough visiting fans from Workington or Torquay in those days, let alone armed crews. Meanwhile, Cardiff were mixing it with many of the most notorious gangs from around the country who supported teams that played in the old Second Division. The result was predictable. From all around South Wales, those with a penchant for violence made for Ninian Park, meaning that Cardiff's infamy was established early on.

Once the Swans began their rapid ascent of the leagues there were soon residents of the west who were eager to rival that reputation, with the result that a pattern was established that was to make matches more high profile off the pitch than on it. Matters arguably reached their nadir before Christmas 1993 with the infamous battle in the grandstand at Ninian Park. By the mid 1990s away fans were banned, and even when the ban was later relaxed, away fans were transported in cordons reminiscent of scenes from the miners' strike of a decade or so earlier.

The potential for violence even spilled over into the support for the Welsh national team. Many decent Welsh fans recall with shame and annoyance the night when Wales took on Iceland at the Vetch in 1981 when factions of rival South Wales support spent almost the entire match singing Swansea and Cardiff songs rather than getting behind their country. In subsequent years an away trip with Wales has been full of potential pitfalls for followers of the Swans, or any of the other Welsh clubs for that matter, as an element of Cardiff support seeks to assert their self proclaimed superior 'patriotism' in a manner unlikely to win friends and influence people. Indeed, one of the most annoying sights for Wales supporters (including, in fairness many Cardiff fans) is that of Bluebirds fans turning up for international fixtures in club shirts. When the opposition play in blue, the utter idiocy of these alleged fans is highlighted to the full. Sadly the Welsh FA have sat back and done little to combat this tendency, apparently oblivious to the discomfort of fans of the many other clubs of Wales who don't seek to turn international occasions into a platform for internal rivalry.

Yet there are plenty of decent supporters on either side of the Swansea versus Cardiff divide who find the poisonous aspects of the rivalry an anathema. It should not be forgotten that when the Swans faced extinction in the winter of 1985-86, ordinary Cardiff fans dug deep into their pockets and gave generously to the Swans appeal buckets at Ninian Park. When all is said and done, the majority of Swansea and Cardiff fans have an awful lot in common. They both prefer football in a country where the media has traditionally concentrated on rugby. They both support their local team in preference to Premiership giants. They support the same national team.

The majority of fans on both sides are, one suspects, capable of keeping the relationship between the teams in context. It is after all a sporting rivalry that should be intense on the field, but need not be civil war off it. There is after all, no longstanding political or religious background to the rivalry however much some on either side attempt to pretend otherwise. Players such as John Toshack, Alan Curtis and Robbie James have worn both clubs' colours with some success and respect from the fans. Yet for some on the terraces, a mature view seems impossible, and as with all fundamentalists, hatred becomes all-consuming. It seems that to this element, the Swans finishing ahead of Cardiff in the league table represents success, even if this was in the lower reaches of the Third Division. That parochial rivalry has plumbed such depths says much about the self-image of both clubs.

Nobody expects Swans fans to love Cardiff City. They are our local rivals, and an element of genuine competitive edge is natural. Yet to fixate about a rival is surely unhealthy, particularly when the rival is so underachieving. Obsessive hatred gives legitimacy to many Cardiff fans' delusions of grandeur. Yet the Bluebirds' history, particularly in the last 25 years, features little to inspire undue jealousy. For the most part of that period they have been a struggling lower division club with a ground well past it's sell by date. This is not Real Madrid or Manchester United. When rivalry spills over into disorder on the streets then something is seriously amiss. Schadenfreude is one thing, riots quite another.

Solutions to the problem are not simple, but the cycle of violence has been damaging to both clubs. Many potential supporters must have been put off by lurid rumours and images on television screens such as those broadcast in December 1993. In one sense there were probably those in the boardrooms at both The Vetch and Ninian Park who quietly breathed a sigh of relief when fortune declared a temporary cessation of hostilities.

10. Any way up

Few seasons have produced such conflicting emotions for Swansea City fans as that of 1999-2000. For 51 years the Swans had not won a championship. Even in the Toshack era we had never finished top of the pile, king of the heap. Suddenly, and somewhat unexpectedly, it happened. Yet when that elusive championship arrived, the overall feelings were mixed, and there was not a little disbelief. Rather like the serious musician who has made number one in the charts through playing on a novelty record, we seemed to have achieved a desired end by less than satisfactory means.

There had been little in the way of transfer activity over the summer. Dave O'Gorman had returned to the League of Wales, perhaps slightly unlucky in that he had frequently performed effectively, but with the emergence of Stuart Roberts and Jason Price, the club seemed well blessed in the wide right position. The only inward movement had also involved the League of Wales, as Hollins signed Bangor striker Tommy Mutton for £20,000.

The season started brightly enough, with four wins out of five league fixtures and a further victory over Millwall, this time over two legs in the League Cup. However, two of those league victories typified the forthcoming season. The opening home fixture against Carlisle had seen a promising opening and the team take the lead. However, there was a failure to score more when on top, and a nervous close as the team defended increasingly deeply and allowed themselves to come under late pressure. This prompted more than a few memories of games in the second half of the previous season. On the other hand, the victory away at Macclesfield had seen the home team lead and fail to ram home their advantage, while the Swans stole the game against the run of play with two late goals from Richie Appleby.

Bearing in mind the lack of team strengthening over the summer, perhaps it was not surprising that the performances bore more than a passing resemblance to the previous campaign. If anything, it was arguable that the team looked rather less threatening as target man Julian Alsop totally lost form and struggled to even achieve convincing attempts on goal, let alone get on the score-sheet.

As if to emphasise that the bright form of August was as ephemeral as the West Wales summer sun, September saw the clouds gather. Following defeat at home to early pacesetters Barnet, the team gradually slipped down the league table, and the failure to strengthen the squad over the close season caused ripples of discontent amongst supporters reminiscent of the Doug Sharpe era. The ambitious talk of the time when the company formerly known as Silver Shield took over the club, and even the expenditure afforded to Alan Cork, now seemed as if from another age.

Discontent over team performance was hardly the worst aspect of crowd behaviour to concern the club. The uglier side of the support had come to the fore with racist chanting providing discomfort and embarrassment to the majority of the home crowd during the 3-1 win over Southend. This prompted some fans to write to club seeking positive action. In fairness, the club did respond positively in the next home fixture with a high profile campaign of anti-racist posters, but sadly the problem was not solved quite so easily, and little further action taken. Once again one was left with the uncomfortable thought that this was a club stuck in a time-warp that could have been doing more to clean up its act.

Whether consciously or not, the Swans did strike a minor blow against the racists by signing Jamaican international Walter Boyd. A legend in his own country, 'Blacka' Boyd had played a major part in the Reggae Boyz qualifying campaign for the 1998 World Cup, but a rather less prominent role once they were there. A television documentary prior to the finals had portrayed him as mercurially talented but liable to unpredictable behaviour. The Jamaicans' Brazilian coach, Rene Simoes appeared to have reservations about his ability at the very highest level. Whether he could set the Third Division alight would be an interesting question.

Certainly Boyd did not appear to lack confidence, stating that his aim was to break the club's all-time scoring record. When he got off the mark within minutes on his debut against Rotherham, and followed it with a delicious chip for a match clinching second, it seemed that the Swans might have found the answer to their goal-scoring problems. However, if we were expecting a larger than life character to light up the season we were to be disappointed. While Boyd provided some neat touches in the following matches, and a further goal against Exeter, it became obvious that he was unlikely to single-handedly transform the team, and his body language increasingly suggested that here was a man wondering what he - or more probably his agent - had got himself into.

The main difficulty was the side's style of play, which appeared to take as a role model the Arsenal of late period George Graham. That team had been built around a solid defence and workmanlike midfield, relying on the ability of Ian Wright to score goals out of the most limited of opportunities. Arsenal had won a number of trophies with this approach based on organisation and perspiration rather than inspiration, but they were popular with few except the most hardened Gooner.

Possibly Hollins envisaged Boyd filling the Wright role in his own increasingly workmanlike team, but the Jamaican appeared ill-suited to the part. Anybody who had followed the build up to the 1998 World Cup would have been aware of the free-flowing philosophy of the Jamaican team, who clearly drew inspiration more from the 1970 Brazilians than George Graham's grim mechanicals. Had he received more sympathetic support and intelligent service then we might have seen the best of Boyd. Whilst the crowd could easily differentiate between the sprightly Jamaican and the tall lumbering figure of Julian Alsop, it seemed that too often the players on the pitch could not, as a series of hopeful long balls aimed toward Walter's head testified.

Unfortunately the men most likely to play to feet and complement the Jamaican's strengths seemed shadows of their former selves. Richie Appleby was fast proving himself the enigma's enigma, rarely producing the exciting runs that had thrilled the crowd in previous seasons, while the negative aspects of his persona were apparently winning out over his undoubted natural talent. It says much that for many fans the most memorable moment of Appleby's season was his sending off at Cwmbran in an FAW Trophy match for kicking the ball at the Assistant Referee not once, but twice.

Similarly, Jonathan Coates was proving that Appleby was not the Swans' only enigma. While not replicating Appleby's petulance, and frequently the purveyor of good performances, Coates had become deeply frustrating to watch. The promise of his skilful attacking play under Molby had disappeared and only resurfaced fitfully. Too often he seemed reluctant to take on his man, and the penetrative runs of just a year or two earlier took second place to the safety first ball. Had he receded into his shell as a result of damaged confidence? Or was he playing to orders, substituting solid professionalism for his youthful flair? Was the new Coates a direct result of Hollins' apparent desire to construct an efficient disciplined team?

Add in that Stuart Roberts spent much of the season sidelined by injury, while Steve Watkin was not producing the goals he had scored the previous season, and attacking options were not plentiful. A poor performance in a scoreless draw at home to league newcomers Cheltenham prompted chants of 'Hollins out' from parts of the crowd. The board responded with the dreaded vote of confidence, and also announced that the club had incurred a loss of some £850,000 during their first year in charge. The crowd had dwindled to the hard core of three and a half thousand and the promise of the early season results seemed a long time before.

For whatever reason, the performance in the 3-1 win over Halifax in the next home fixture was described by some as not only the best of the season, but the best for some years. Perhaps it was no coincidence that Appleby and Coates provided performances that rolled back the clock. Optimists pointed out that Molby's team had started a run to the play-offs at a similar stage in the season. If the eventual outcome was to surpass even that achievement, hopes that the win would prompt a reversion to a more open style of football were premature. The team returned to a more conservative approach the following week when drawing at Shrewsbury, and the chants for Hollins' head returned.

Walter Boyd had aimed to break records when he joined, and in a home fixture against Darlington in November he succeeded in carving his place in not only club, but world football history. Unfortunately, in a season when the team set new statistical standards, this one was best forgotten, although its continued presence in the record books appears guaranteed. Coming on as substitute, Boyd was involved in a minor fracas with a defender, and saw a red card before the whistle had re-started play. As the dismissal was officially recorded at nil seconds, it is difficult to see how it can ever be beaten.

Rumours abounded as to John Hollins' job security, and once again, football's perversity came to the fore as the team not only won their next match at Chester, but went on to break a club record by winning nine in succession. Mid-table mediocrity was turned into league leadership in a matter of weeks. Yet had a Chester player not missed a simple chance from two yards out in the dying seconds, some believed that the club would have been seeking the fifth manager of the Ninth Floor era.

While the wins were welcome, there remained a sense of incredulity amongst certain sections of support. The team seemed well organised from the back forward, but posed little in the way of attacking threat. Had the teams of Harry Griffiths or John Toshack put together this run, few would have been surprised. In the case of the present team, many supporters were left rubbing their eyes as single goal victory followed single goal victory. Some fans thought we were riding our luck, and that it would soon run out. In fact it was to be almost a year before payback came in spades.

Despite the run coming to an end with a 2-1 loss at Southend, the victories kept coming. Perhaps the home win over struggling Chester, achieved when coming from a goal behind in injury time after a poor performance, was proof that some eternal force was with the team. Sky Television visited the Vetch for the visit of Northampton who dominated the match, but lost 4-1. On the basis that Hollins was one of Napoleon's lucky generals, promotion seemed a certainty. Even when the team hit a sticky patch and took only four points from six matches, their rivals also wavered. Nerves were settled by successive wins over Easter, although again luck smiled when a potential Torquay equaliser came back off the bar in the final minute with Roger Freestone helpless. Consequently, the Swans were left to beat struggling Exeter at the Vetch to clinch promotion. Over 10,000 packed the ground as a Grecian team featuring former Vetch hero John Cornforth was despatched 3-0. Jonathon Coates scored with a spectacular shot, while Walter Boyd contributed perhaps his best game in a Swansea shirt, having a goal disallowed and generally keeping the crowd on their feet with a series of tricks and turns.

The result left the Swans top of the table with one match to play – away at second placed Rotherham, who had also won to clinch promotion. If the Yorkshire side won, they would finish top, but a draw would be good enough for Hollins' team to clinch the club's first championship trophy since the Third Division South was won in 1948. Over 2,000 Swans fans travelled to South Yorkshire on a hot early summer afternoon. Anybody who thought that this fixture would be a relaxed celebratory kick about between two already promoted sides was in for a rude shock. Walking to the ground, there was a menace in the air that went well beyond anticipation of the tense events that were to unfold on the pitch. Inside the packed ground it became obvious that the championship mattered badly to both sets of supporters.

The match itself was a tight affair with both sides creating chances, but as the game approached injury time with no score, it seemed the Swans had done enough. Little did we know quite how long the game was to hang in the balance. When Jason Price was brought down in the penalty area with around a minute left on the clock there seemed little doubt that the championship was on its way to South Wales. Matthew Bound sent the ball rocketing into the net with explosive force, and that seemed to be that. Instead, what followed helped taint a day of victory.

For reasons that might charitably be described as excitement, a few hundred Swans fans spilled onto the pitch to celebrate. After the inevitable hold up, it was apparent that thousands of Rotherham fans had also now encroached onto the touchlines. Whether this was to acclaim their promotion-winning heroes at the final whistle, or to get at their Welsh counterparts is a moot point. Rotherham had been reduced to nine men by sendings-off, and as they needed two goals with less than two minutes to play, the destiny of the championship seemed settled. Surely the sensible course was for the referee to direct play toward the players' tunnel and blow for time. Blow the referee did, but this time for a debateable penalty to Rotherham. Bizarrely, the Rotherham fans chose this moment to invade the pitch. The referee led the players off, but not before Steve Jones had been attacked by a Rotherham fan.

Whether the referee was hoping to appease the home crowd by awarding an equalising penalty, only he knows. Applying the rules strictly is one thing, but surely a little discretion is called for if there is the genuine risk of injury. Like so much else that afternoon, the pantomime that injury time had become appeared avoidable. Eventually the police restored order, and the few remaining seconds played out. Regardless of Rotherham's equalising goal, we were champions! Yet while it was a wonderful moment to see Nick Cusack lift the trophy, the atmosphere had become so poisonous that celebrations were accompanied by a dread feeling as to whether Rotherham fans might seek revenge on either the team or its support.

Events surrounding the last couple of minutes of play took the edge off what should have been one of the best moments for Swans' supporters in some years. However, this was nothing to the feeling of shock that hit most of us when we opened our Sunday newspapers and read of the death of Terry Coles. It seemed that fate had decreed that even success for Swansea City was not to be the cause of unequivocal celebration.

If events off the pitch muted the celebratory mood, there were also unanswered questions surrounding matters on it. Deep down, many supporters couldn't really believe that we had won the championship. Perhaps this was a harsh judgement on a team that had defended well and seemed to possess a good spirit. The team had created club records for both successive league wins and clean sheets, and boasted a defensive record that was the best in the Nationwide League. The downside had been the lack of attacking potency. Perhaps this factor more than anything else did not endear the team or its management to supporters in the manner of the teams that narrowly missed out under Burrows or Molby. It could be argued that Swansea fans had been spoilt down the years and had unrealistic expectations of the team playing the 'beautiful game'. However, even leaving aside the issue of whether this was feasible in the Third Division at the turn of the Millennium, it should be said Hollins' team had produced a tangible success where their more entertaining predecessors had failed.

Yet while few supporters looked a gift championship in the mouth, and there were genuine celebrations come the season's end, the reality was that there had been few truly convincing performances, and genuine doubts existed as to how good the team really were. The feeling after leaving Millmoor that evening was uncannily similar to leaving a shop where the assistant has inadvertently handed you too much change. Discussions in the aftermath centred on the improvements that it seemed were inevitable if the team were to compete at a higher level. If our hearts cheered a rare championship win, then our heads could see a rocky road ahead if the team were not strengthened. Was John Hollins an expert organiser who had got the best out of a limited group of players, or had he stifled instinctive talent? Had we just been plain lucky? Any which way, it seemed something would have to change. Now was the time for the board to show that the statements of ambition made at the time of takeover were not empty promises.

*   *   *

The death of Terry Coles had once again drawn attention to the behaviour of certain supporter factions, and raised issues as to the policing of football matches. Sadly, it highlighted the fact that despite alleged better crowd behaviour at matches, improvements to stadia and changes in police approaches, somebody could still go to a football match and lose their life. Perhaps the worst aspect of the incident was that it seemed so unnecessary and so avoidable.

Terry Coles had travelled with friends in a minibus from Swansea to the game. He was a long-term Swansea fan, season ticket holder and had no record of being involved in trouble at matches. Along with hundreds of other Swans fans he had enjoyed a few pre-match drinks in Rotherham, where there had been little separation of fans before the match, before making his way to the ground.

Outside Millmoor, away fans were directed to their seats at the far end of the ground. The stadium is an old style football ground that had been upgraded by the addition of seats on terraces in the wake of the Taylor

Report and lies in a dingy part of Rotherham, surrounded on two sides by scrap yards. From the main entrance the away end is accessed via Millmoor Lane, an alley that leads along the back of a stand. At its immediate entrance, the lane is overlooked by both a section of terracing occupied by home fans, and the rear garden of the Millmoor public house.

Reports at the time suggested that a group of Swansea fans were passing down the lane when they were ambushed by Rotherham fans standing on the vantage points of terrace and pub garden, who began to bombard them with missiles. In 'military' terms the position of the home fans would surely have been considered a huge advantage. Some Swansea fans retaliated, and there were reports of a full builders' skip in the vicinity providing ammunition. The police moved horses into the lane to move the Swansea fans along. During the chaos, Terry Coles blundered into the path of a police horse that reared, striking him a number of blows that caused his death.

The subsequent Coroner's Inquest arrived at a verdict of Accidental Death, and the main issues highlighted by press reports of the hearing appeared to centre on the immediate aspects of the collision. Whether the verdict was a fair one is matter of contention, but in one sense is irrelevant, as some of the broader issues appeared to attract little comment. Much of the attention at the Inquest seems to have been focused firstly on the level of alcohol in Terry Coles' bloodstream, and secondly on allegations by the Police as to his involvement in the missile throwing, denied by witnesses who were with him.

Whatever the truth of those allegations and denials, the immediate circumstances of the incident should not be allowed to obscure serious questions about the organisation and preparation for the match. As an ordinary peaceful and law abiding Swansea fan who walked down Millmoor Lane that day and felt the tension in the air as we passed through the restricted space between pub and terrace, and subsequently imagined the presence of a rearing horse, I could not help be struck by the thought that many more people might have got caught in a potentially fatal situation through no fault of their own.

At the outset it should be said that any missile throwing or other violent or threatening behaviour that occurred that afternoon cannot be condoned. While it seems from reports that Rotherham fans were the original aggressors in the particular situation, this did not justify retaliation. Unfortunately, as is referred to elsewhere in this book, there is an element of the Swansea support that has earned a reputation for being involved in crowd disturbances. This socially unacceptable group could cost the club whether by way of fines, or through the frightening away of mainstream support. Similarly, as long as the club enjoys a 'reputation' in certain circles, its supporters will be targeted, particularly in away fixtures. For the true football diehard this can lead to double jeopardy as they become the target of opposing fans, and are also sometimes treated as a job lot by police forces content to throw in the hooligans with innocent bystanders.

Yet even allowing for the possible bad behaviour of certain elements of the Swans' support, the circumstances at Rotherham posed other questions. Indeed, the very fact that some parts of the Swans' following did have something of a colourful reputation might have highlighted some of these issues. Whilst observers from a distance might have not thought the fixture a potential hotbed of hate, the idea that this was to be some sort of carnival of football was surely wide of the mark. This was always going to be a tense title decider played before a sell-out crowd in a town that was in the centre of the former industrial heartlands, featuring visitors whose support included a less than savoury element. Talk among fans surrounded the various threats that had appeared on internet message boards in the week leading up to the game.

With this backdrop, the question occurs as to whether there should have been a higher degree of segregation of fans before the game. At the very least, might Swans fans have been routed differently toward their seats, instead of being guided through an obvious ambush point? Further, were the rumours true of there having been crates of bottles in the pub garden and a full builders skip left in situ, thus providing a ready supply of ammunition? All these questions seemed to be begged even before one considered whether it was wise to send a police horse into a restricted and crowded space when missiles were flying. Many of us who were wholly without malevolent intent look back on walking the potential gauntlet of Millmoor Lane and shuddered at the thought that we too might have arrived in the wrong place at the wrong time.

Many of us who had regularly attended matches over the years had often wondered whether the routine crushes that occurred in and around football grounds, and the manner in which police horses were sometimes deployed, were entirely safe. Hillsborough had provided a grotesque answer to the first part of the question. Had we now received an answer to the second?

We looked for reassurance from the authorities that some form of lesson had been learnt, but found little comfort in the press reports of official statements at the time of the Inquest. While it was feasible that the South Yorkshire Police were being reticent due to an ongoing claim in the civil courts brought on behalf of Terry Coles' dependants, the tone of the police responses was not encouraging. There is no doubt that the police frequently have a difficult job to do at football matches. Yet regardless of the outcomes of the various court proceedings, as an ordinary fan who attended the match I remain far from convinced that the game had been properly managed and correct judgements made.

Some four and a half years later there was at least some light at the end of the tunnel. An investigation into events surrounding the match by the West Yorkshire Police following a referral to the Independent Police Complaints Commission upheld complaints against three police officers for a "failure of duty". Two of the officers had retired, and the equivalent of a verbal warning was given to a senior officer. The South Yorkshire Police continued to defend the compensation claim, but acknowledged that the report criticised aspects of management on the day.

It would be nice to think that in the aftermath of somebody being killed at a football match that there might be a little reflection by those involved and lessons learnt. The fall out from Rotherham did not exactly encourage positive feelings that this was the case. The police force involved gave the impression of being mainly concerned with avoiding blame, whilst groups of Swansea supporters were soon involved in trouble the following season. Meanwhile the club did little to actively deal with a problem that could be as unpleasant and potentially dangerous for decent Swans' fans as it was for the police or the opposition.

British football had seemingly undergone a radical transformation post Hillsborough. The made-over image suggested that grounds were now safe and crowds well behaved. Yet far below the shiny new world of the Premiership, in the aftermath of Rotherham, it was difficult to be optimistic that anything had truly changed.

*   *   *

If the Swans' season had come to a close in the sunshine of South Yorkshire, there was still plenty of football to be played elsewhere before the close season. The global circus of world football travelled on, and this time around the Swans would play a minor part, as Roger Freestone was selected to play for Wales in a hastily arranged friendly against Brazil at the Millennium Stadium. With a hitherto concealed entrepreneurial air, the Welsh FA set up the fixture at short notice. Unlike their English counterparts, they pegged prices at an affordable level so that thousands of Welsh children had the opportunity to see Rivaldo and company in the flesh. Roger excelled himself, producing a number of saves that helped keep the score to a respectable 3-0 against a strong Brazilian team. While most home fans were hardly cheering when Cafu sent a wickedly swerving volley into the Welsh net, the skill was breathtaking and left those who were there with a memory of witnessing something special.

The international focus shifted to the Low Countries a few weeks later as Belgium and Holland co-hosted Euro 2000. The event featured some fine football, and also highlighted the growing European influence on the British game. Many of the stars of the tournament played in the Premiership, although it should be said that very few of them appeared in the England team. Yet if the tournament brought into focus the reliance of the Premiership on foreign players to boost its skill and entertainment levels, the mere presence of so many players, particularly from the production lines of France and Holland, evidenced one of the greatest contemporary influences of Europe on British football – the Bosman ruling. The effect of Bosman competed with the Champions League as to which had the most distorting influence on English football.

The European Court of Justice decision in the Bosman case was handed down in September 1995 and was to have a cataclysmic effect on European transfer dealings. The irony was that while the decision was undoubtedly morally correct in helping dismantle the antiquated Belgian transfer system, it was also to blow apart the rather less restrictive - and some would say better balanced - systems in other European countries including Britain. In applying the principles of general labour law to the employment of footballers, the decision had ramifications for the British and European club scene that were both revolutionary and destabilising.

British players were now free to move at will come the end of their contracts, even if their existing clubs were prepared to match terms offered elsewhere. The Bosman decision took away the bargaining hand of the selling club in obtaining a fee for an out of contract player. Consequently, the pressure to sell an unsettled player during the final year of his contract became almost irresistible. Incentives to illicitly unsettle a player were manifest. While there was the limited exception of a tribunal compensation scheme for younger players, the power of a club to retain a player, even by offering reasonable terms was undermined.

It had always been difficult for a club to hang on to an unsettled player, but at least in the past transfer fees provided a form of compensation. Although one longer term effect of the Bosman ruling was to be the partial disappearance of transfer fees between lower division British clubs, the reality for many smaller clubs was that it was increasingly difficult to build a team from scratch via youth products, or to ensure survival of the club through player sales. A player in his final year of a contract is in an extremely strong position when coveted by other clubs. While football has had to adjust to the new landscape, it would be naïve to think that there has not been any effect on competition in a sporting sense.

Certainly for a club such as Swansea City, who had a reputation for developing young players, the ruling was not good news. To place in context, if Bosman had been in force at the time that Alan Curtis was transferred to Leeds, it is highly doubtful that the Swans would have received the record fee that helped team strengthening in his wake. The club might spend time and money on developing a young player but were no longer guaranteed a transfer fee if he was to move on. Bigger clubs could wait in the wings, often unsettling a promising young player, who could then be snapped up for a minimal fee. In an increasingly commercial environment, some clubs began to question whether having a youth development strategy was justified economically. It was ironic that a decision ostensibly designed to promote greater competition and fairness in the labour market might have the effect of lessening competition on the field, and possibly limiting opportunities for greater numbers of young players to receive specialist coaching. Many football administrators called 'foul' and argued that football was a special case.

Yet it was hardly surprising that football was being treated as a business by the European institutions. The money generated by the major clubs of Europe was huge, and there had been a trend across the continent, in particular in England to seek to raise money through the financial markets. Fortunes were made through shrewd manipulation of the football business. Football could hardly claim that sport should be given preferential treatment while at the same time acting as an out-and-out branch of the entertainment industry. It seemed that big time football wanted both to have its cake and eat it. It was always too much to hope that football's administrators might take a step back at this stage and ask the basic philosophical questions of whether the game saw itself as a sport or business, community asset or city plaything. There certainly was little let-up in football's new commercial approach. At every turn both UEFA and the Football Association seemed unable to slow down the process.

If Bosman had changed the transfer system beyond all recognition, Europe was also causing distortions to the domestic leagues across the continent through the knock on effects of Champions League participation. The monies earned from participation in the later stages were capable of transforming a club's finances, leaving domestic rivals well behind. As the clubs that qualified for the League in the first place tended to be larger and richer, this further polarised financial clout. From being a bonus competition theoretically open to all to qualify, European competition was now helping perpetuate a self-contained elite who dominated and exorcised any sense of genuine competition within many participating countries. The days of Nottingham Forest and Ipswich Town winning European trophies now seemed like ancient history. Salt was rubbed into wounds at the Vetch as the club's opportunity to qualify for Europe had dwindled.

Yet while Europe has had a distorting effect on British domestic football through both the effects of the Bosman ruling and Champions League riches, it also provides other examples that might act as an antidote to what some supporters see as an over-commercial approach to football. In Germany, clubs are often part of larger sporting associations who are effectively owned by their members. While there has been some relaxation of the rules to enable the professional football sections of sporting clubs to raise money on the open market, the members still retain a majority shareholding. In any circumstances, the control of the clubs cannot ultimately pass from the people who have its genuine interests at heart - the members. This is combined with a rigorous licensing system that requires a club's financial plan to be scrutinised by the authorities. The upshot is a system that encouraged openness and accountability while it is highly unlikely that a German club could be hijacked by an unscrupulous asset stripper or opportunistic businessman.

Similarly, many French teams are also either largely owned by their members or municipalities, and again, while there have been concessions to the need to raise additional funding on the market, the ownership structure of many French clubs does not allow them to stray too far from their primary purpose as sporting institutions. Might it be no coincidence that France has also been prolific in its production of young players?

English and Welsh football has arrived at a stage where the current administration of the clubs has left the majority riddled with debt despite the income into the game being at record levels. On the field, questions are raised as to how genuinely open and competitive the league is. Fans, who are the economic lifeblood of the game, have had little say in shaping the course of events. Few British club chairmen and directors have traditionally been directly accountable to supporters. As the commercial aspects of football ran amok, many fans in Britain began to ask whether there was a better way of doing things. While the historical background and development of clubs in countries such as Germany and France means that exact replication of their ownership structures might not be either possible or appropriate, many supporters began to wonder whether similar ends could be achieved through slightly different means.

It can also be argued that the shakers and movers of Brussels and Strasbourg might be more kindly disposed toward football if clubs were principally community based sporting institutions as opposed to stock market quoted money-making devices. As the market driven experiment of British football headed toward the rocks the opportunity was to arise to steer many British clubs into a different direction. If this all seemed very distant to Swansea City over the summer of the year 2000, subsequent events vindicated those who were sceptical over the long term sustainability of football's dash for cash. Alternative ownership structures, and a very different philosophical stance toward the place of football clubs in the wider world, were to become very much on the agenda. Events at the Vetch Field were to place the club in the front line of this movement.

11. Trouble in store

As Swansea City celebrated a championship and promotion, South Wales rivals Cardiff City were heading in the opposite direction, relegated back to the Third Division after a single season in the Second. In May 2000 one could be forgiven for having thought that the two clubs were heading for very different futures, with the all-white side of South Wales in the ascendant. After all, hadn't our then current owners talked of Premiership potential in a brand new stadium, while the Bluebirds had once again flattered to deceive? Yet by the time the season kicked off this analysis was open to question. On the one hand the lack of on-field strengthening at the Vetch engendered doubts as to whether the Swans could survive in the higher division. On the other, the gloom over Ninian Park had dissipated following the purchase of the club by former Wimbledon owner Sam Hammam, who arrived making promises of massive investment.

In many respects Hammam represented another face of club ownership, the rich super-benefactor. This was hardly a new phenomenon. Elton John had bankrolled Watford's rise to prominence, while Jack Walker had purchased a Premiership championship for small town Blackburn. The main difference was that both these men were life-long supporters of clubs generally considered to be unfashionable, and indulged their passion with money made in other walks of life. In contrast, the money that Hammam brandished at Cardiff came from his involvement with Wimbledon. He came to a club, with which he had no previous allegiance, on the basis of their commercial potential. Indeed, Hammam's only previous connection with Cardiff had been to cause a minor furore amongst Bluebird fans when he proposed moving Wimbledon to the National Stadium.

Had Hammam taken over at just about any other club in Britain, most Swans fans would have reacted philosophically. However, when he moved into Sloper Road to take over the Swans' traditional rivals, his activities couldn't be ignored in the west. Sam was hardly a shrinking violet when it came to seeking publicity. When that publicity centred on Cardiff City, the reaction of many Swans fans involved boiling blood at high pressure. The combination of Sam Hammam and Cardiff City was a premonition of hell to many folk west of Bridgend. Whilst it was unsurprising that the Cardiff-based media were receptive to the new owner, and enthusiastically endorsed the take-over, little thought appeared to be given to sensitivities outside the capital.

On one level the enthusiasm was understandable, as Hammam did promise to bring additional funding to an under-performing club, and could claim some level of success with his former charges. However, when subjected to closer scrutiny, Hammam's record at Wimbledon was not as straightforward as it seemed. He had been involved with the club during their Swansea-like rise through the divisions and FA Cup win.

However, those successes had largely been achieved in a very different financial environment, and it was likely that to repeat the feat would require rather more substantial investment than had been needed in the mid-1980s.

Further, the Dons' rise had rested to a large extent on the abilities of manager Dave Bassett, and the abrasive style of play he employed. The fairy tale of Wimbledon never struck the chord that it might with football's romantics, largely due to the club's style of play. Many neutral fans' admiration of their exploits was tempered by the perception of the team as hooligans who had invaded the pitch. This may have contributed to Wimbledon's crowds never matching their achievements. They were unable to attract viable support at a time when other London clubs were regularly selling out their stadia. Perhaps the 'Crazy Gang' image so wholeheartedly endorsed by Sam Hammam just didn't appeal to the leafy middle class suburbs of South West London. He had ultimately presided over a show that in box office terms would have closed after its first week on Broadway.

There were also more basic reasons, possibly shared by the more thoughtful Bluebirds fans to be sceptical of Sam Hammam. While he had presided over success at Wimbledon, some of his decisions when in charge and the manner of his leaving caused disquiet amongst the 'Dons' faithful fans. It appeared that Sam had sold the club near the top of football's bull market, making a significant profit on his original investment. Also, he had left the club homeless, having sold their Plough Lane ground. While it can be argued he was correct in his assessment that the ground had no future as a top level football stadium, his mooted solutions to Wimbledon's search for a new home had caused resentment amongst Dons' fans when he proposed moving the club, franchise-style, to both Dublin and, ironically, Cardiff.

Sam had often spoken of his love for Wimbledon, but fans of that club were to increasingly feel that his was no love supreme; it certainly didn't seem to get in the way of a good deal. In this instance cynics might conclude that 'love' was worth a reported £24 million. Predictably, it was not long before Sam was waxing lyrical about his latest acquisition. As Tina Turner once sang: "What's love got to do with it?"

Yet all of this might not have mattered terribly to the fans of Swansea City, had it not been for Sam's sudden espousal of a form of Welsh nationalism. It seemed that within minutes of crossing the Severn Bridge he was telling everybody who would listen that Cardiff City were now the club of Wales, and that all red blooded Welshmen should join his crusade. Over the summer months Wales was bombarded with claims that Cardiff City could represent the nation on a journey into the Premiership and beyond. Not only that, but apparently Cardiff could be to Wales what Barcelona were to Catalunya. Such statements revealed a questionable level of knowledge of both contemporary Welsh and European history.

As noted earlier Wales is divided by a number of factors, many historical, but likely to be with us for the foreseeable future. Geographically, lines of communication ran east to west, while north to south links are spartan. Language also divides the country, roughly on an east-west basis. There are also growing political and economic divides between the relatively affluent areas near the English border and most of the remainder of Wales. The irony of a city that never voted for the Welsh Assembly benefiting economically from its establishment is not lost on many outside the south east.

If these factors led one to doubt how much knowledge Hammam had of his adopted homeland, the comparison of Cardiff City to FC Barcelona exhibited a superficiality that was downright insulting. Even the most rudimentary knowledge of the Spanish Civil War reveals that thousands of Catalans died in that struggle, while many more were killed, imprisoned or exiled in the aftermath of Franco's dictatorship. The Camp Nou came to represent a haven for the expression of Catalan identity. Barca was regarded as more than an ordinary football club and the attempts by Sam Hammam to compare Cardiff City were laughably shallow.

More thoughtful fans may have also raised questions as to quite how far reaching Hammam's vision might be, and the implications for Welsh football as a whole. Football's entrepreneurial class increasingly appeared to be envisaging a Europe of the regions, with each area represented by a major club. Such visions dovetailed neatly with Sam Hammam's ambitions for Cardiff to be the surrogate Welsh national team. From the point of view of Swans fans, there was a danger that if Cardiff City assumed the mantle of regional super-club, their own team would become something of a local sideshow. Rather as in American baseball, or indeed the current re-invention of Welsh club rugby, other teams in the area become mere feeders. Swansea City, Newport County and others would become little more than junior teams, an afterthought to the main event. As we saw when considering American sports, this would make perfect sense within the concept of football as a branch of the entertainment industry.

Sam Hammam's involvement with Cardiff City raised a number of far reaching questions as to how we view professional football clubs. Firstly, is it desirable for one man to have complete control of a club? Secondly, is it desirable for a complete outsider to buy a club with which he has no previous connection, purely because of its commercial potential? Thirdly, if success is purchased for a club by such an outsider, is it then truly the club and its supporters' success in any event, or do the fans merely share vicariously in somebody else's victory? Moreover, are we content to see our country or nation merely reduced to the status of a commercial franchise? Finally, do we see our clubs as purely profit making corporations or do they have a deeper resonance in their communities?

If there were profound questions that went to the soul of Welsh sport posed by Hammam's takeover and ambitions for Cardiff City, there were few actively asking them either amongst their support or in sections of the Welsh media. Moreover, at a more mundane level there were practical questions that occurred, such as quite how Hammam's lofty ambitions were to be funded. Swansea City fans had already learnt of the price to be paid when financial reality didn't equate with grand ambition, and many were imbued with a certain degree of scepticism. However, Cardiff City's supporters and the local media seemed to buy the new owner's statements at face value. Perhaps the city had become so desperate for success that it did not want to pull back the stone for fear of uncovering a snake. Yet in an age when football has assumed a quasi-religious significance the perhaps even otherwise rational people are prepared to suspend their disbelief when an apparent messiah arrives. For whatever reason, there seemed few dissonant voices in the capital prepared to analyse Hammam's record at Wimbledon beyond a superficial level, or to question what his expressed vision truly meant for either Cardiff City or Welsh sport as a whole.

Hammam's much publicised exhortations for the whole of Wales to get behind his team naturally raised hackles amongst Swansea City fans. On occasions this resulted in racist chanting of questionable accuracy being aimed at the Cardiff chairman. Although much of this could be attributed to stupidity rather than anything more sinister, it did divert attention from the fact that there were more potentially serious reasons to be suspicious of Sam Hammam. Meanwhile, the Swans were hardly in a position to cast the first stone, as the club themselves were the property of a profit seeking organisation. However, the wheels were about to come off this particular enterprise.

*   *   *

The first close season of the new millennium epitomised most of Swansea City's previous existence – much anticipation, but ultimately little delivered. Whatever the reservations about the style of play that had evolved under John Hollins, most fans accepted that the team looked well organised, and that there was a solid base from which to work. However, most realists also recognised that there would be stern challenges offered by the big spenders of the Second Division.

That there was to be a radical step up in the world was evidenced by some of the venues the Swans would visit in the months ahead. Stoke, Reading, Millwall, and Wigan possessed brand-new stadia fit for the Premiership while Notts County had completely rebuilt Meadow Lane to similar standards. Add in the extensively modernised grounds at the likes of Bristol City and Wrexham, and the Vetch appeared to be from a different age. When one also considered the money spent by the likes of Reading and Wigan on their players, it seemed that major changes had taken place in the division in the four seasons that the club had been absent. The Second Division could never be described as 'big time', but there were a number of clubs borrowing clothes from the wardrobe.

The Swans' sole transfer acquisition was Andrew Mumford from

League of Wales Llanelli, a promising youngster but hardly the reinforcement many thought necessary if the team were to compete at the higher level. The squad looked rather thin in places, lacking both experienced cover and options. While the previous season's success had been based on admirable qualities such as organisation, commitment and character, there seemed a distinct lack of creativity and scoring power.

'Sign a striker' became one of the regular refrains at the Vetch in the season's opening weeks. Hollins said that he had players in mind, but the only concrete development was an approach for former Chelsea striker Mark Stein, who many felt was past his sell-by date. For all the fine words of intent, the squad had actually become weaker in the forward department, as both Julian Alsop and Tony Bird had been allowed to leave. In one sense this was no surprise, as neither player had set the world alight the previous season. Alsop had started out as a popular figure, providing genuine ability in the air and focus for the attack. However, he had cut a sorry figure at times in his final season, his confidence seemingly lost as he struggled for goals. Similarly, Tony Bird had enjoyed a bright start to his Swansea career, scoring regularly under Jan Molby. However, Bird had seemed very much a confidence player, and under John Hollins the goals had come less frequently. Whatever the potential merits and drawbacks of either Bird or Alsop in the Second Division, to release both without replacement seemed highly questionable.

Despite the doubts, record season ticket sales evidenced supporter interest, and a healthy crowd of around 8,300 turned out for the opening match at the Vetch against promotion favourites Wigan. Only the churlish would have felt truly disappointed with the scoreless draw against one of the division's big spenders, but when the next two matches also finished 0-0, many fans began to wonder whether we were ever again going to see a goal. Predictions of defensive solidity combined with attacking impotence looked accurate. Even the solid defence disappeared in the next home match as Tresor Lomana Lua-Lua ran the Swans ragged in a 2-0 defeat by Colchester that could have been a lot worse. However, there was little panic at that stage because the African was clearly an exceptional talent, a point emphasised by his subsequent transfer to Newcastle United.

Showing the character that had served them so well previously, the team bounced back to win three of the next four league matches, including a 4-0 hammering of a Luton side that already appeared relegation fodder. They also gave a spirited performance in losing 2-1 at West Bromwich in the League Cup. Those supporters who sat in the away end that night could not help look at the modernised Hawthorns, compare it to the play-off semi-final defeat of seven years earlier, and contrast the fortunes of the clubs in the interim.

If developments at WBA provided food for thought, the visit to Reading's Madejski Stadium was a revelation, and possibly the season's most significant result. The fixture came at the end of a difficult week in which chairman Steve Hamer had either jumped or was pushed from the hot seat. Hamer certainly possessed a sense of timing, for unlike over 1,000 members of the Jack Army, he succeeded in missing a 5-1 defeat, the club's worst league result under Hollins. Until that match there had been signs that the manager's methodical approach could at least ensure mid-table solidity. Suddenly, we were made only too aware that this was a different league to that which we had left.

Many theories have been advanced as to the decline in the clubs fortunes beyond this point. Hamer's allies suggested that the loss of his influence was crucial. It was certainly true that the subsequent turn around in fortunes followed his departure, and that Hamer had enjoyed an apparently good relationship with Hollins. However, whether Hamer could or would have sanctioned the spending that many fans believed necessary to upgrade the team is questionable. Yet the defeat at Reading didn't suggest that this was an unhappy team, distracted by off-field uncertainty. The Swans performed reasonably well in many respects, but were punished by a mix of excellent Reading finishing, and a failure to capitalise on their own chances. They had been undone by superior ability in crucial areas of the field. While Reading had spent heavily on the strike partnership of Butler and Cureton, the Swans hadn't made any significant signings. In this division the better sides took no prisoners. The error of failing to recognise this and strengthen was now put in sharp relief.

It is also possible is that the result affected confidence and infected both the manager and the team with self-doubt. Previously, Hollins had stuck to his guns and not altered his conservative approach. From here on in, it seemed tactics and personnel were changed on an almost weekly basis. Had this been the result of tailoring tactics to combat specific opponents, and results justified such variances, few would have quibbled. As it was, the manager increasingly gave the impression of not knowing his best team or the best tactics to adopt. Possibly this transmitted itself to the players as the performances over the next few weeks seemed to lack the conviction and spirit that had carried the team so far.

In fairness, Hollins was handicapped by long term injuries to a number of key personnel including Jason Smith and Jonathan Coates, while it seemed that some previously key players were struggling to come to terms with the higher division. The mean defence of the previous season was to appear increasingly porous, as the absence of Smith was sorely felt. Meanwhile, his partner Bound suddenly appeared vulnerable against fast and quick-turning opponents. The rocks on which the championship had been built suddenly looked susceptible to erosion.

Equally, whatever his detractors might say, Coates was naturally left-sided, and the failure to adequately replace him was to leave the team looking unbalanced. Whether Hollins failed to recognise the failings or whether the board were not prepared to back his judgement, his claims that the squad were good enough to compete in the division were already looking hollow with less than a third of the season gone.

The club did sign two players during October. Giovanni Savarese, a Venezuelan who had played in the American Major League Soccer arrived alongside David Romo, a French midfielder from Guingamp. Both impressed on their debuts in a 2-1 win against Stoke, providing goal-scoring prowess and creative guile respectively. However, this was to prove a false dawn, as both took time to adjust to the speed and physicality of the English lower divisions.

Following the victory over Stoke in mid-October the club lay in mid-table. However, 11 further league fixtures were to pass before the next victory. Many fans felt that Hollins' employment should have been terminated at this time, as five points out of a possible 33 told its own story. While Savarese began to score on a fairly regular basis, results remained awful, and it was obvious that something would have to change, for by Christmas the club were looking certain for relegation. Alarm bells should have sounded when rock-bottom Oxford won at the Vetch in November, but supporters felt that there was little urgency displayed by the manager or the board.

It seemed that Hollins was now caught in a conundrum: if he played in a highly tight and organised fashion the team couldn't score; if he attempted to be more open and creative they became stretched and vulnerable. While the team were able to grind out a few points from draws, including a remarkable come-back with three goals in the last 15 minutes at Cambridge, the club clearly needed wins if it was to climb out of trouble. Without further strengthening it was difficult to see how this could happen.

One could only surmise that by this stage, owners Ninth Floor and new chairman Neil McClure had despaired of ever turning Swansea City Football Club into a profit making concern, and were looking at means of escape with minimum damage. If they had seriously possessed long-term ambitions for the club, a change of management and influx of new players would surely have been on the agenda. Fans with longer memories recalled how Doug Sharpe had swallowed his pride in replacing Colin Appleton with John Bond in December 1984, and how relegation was averted from a similar position.

The suspicion was that the owners had no such overview. The Morfa project had once again ground to a halt, as club owners and Council couldn't appear to find a way forward. The floating of the club on the money markets - apparently the cause of the dispute that led to Hamer's departure - seemed to have been quietly forgotten. With Hollins either unable or unwilling to bring in fresh blood through Burrows-style wheeling and dealing, the chances were that little would change in the way of playing staff. Many fans believed that an injection of a few experienced second division journeymen might have saved the season, but they were never to find out.

That left matters in the lap of the Gods. If Hollins was hoping for a stroke of luck, he should have known that his number was up as the year ended. Arguably the best performance of the season saw the Swans defeat promotion chasing Walsall 3-1 on Boxing Day, and if that form could have been repeated a few days later at home to Brentford, then the season might yet have been turned around. Hollins must have looked to the skies and despaired as a heavy snowfall prevented the match being played. It seemed that all of the manager's good fortune had been used up the previous season, and that now no deposits remained in the celestial favour bank. Instead, the club was firmly in the hands of mortals, and the portents were not good.

The next fixture at high-flying Wigan was lost, commencing a further sequence that left the Swans with one victory in 22 league matches. The manager might have called it a day early in the New Year, as it was by now obvious that the team were heading in one direction. However, whether through obstinacy or sheer delusion, Hollins hung on. Publicly he continued to proclaim that the season could be turned around, and that the current team and management could do it. Few supporters were convinced. Whether the board would have backed a replacement by that point is doubtful, but we were never to find out.

Indeed, Luton had revived and given themselves a chance of survival by employing former Wimbledon manager Joe Kinnear. The teams met in a six-pointer at Kenilworth Road, where a dreadful defensive display resulted in a 5-3 defeat despite a Savarese hat-trick. February became the cruellest month, yielding only a single point from six fixtures. The Gods now decided to call in the good luck overdraft run up during the previous season. With an almost poetic sense of timing, the Swans played at Northampton almost exactly a year after having beaten Chester with two injury time goals. In an eerily mirror-like reversal of that game, they led at Sixfields as the game entered stoppage-time, only to concede twice in two minutes. At that point most supporters lost all hope.

The goal at Northampton had been scored by Nicolas Fabiano, a player who had arrived on loan from Paris St Germain, along with compatriot Matthias Verchave. Rather like David Romo, the pair seemed skilful, but not necessarily the players to get the club out of trouble at the lower end of the English Second Division. It was also questionable whether the team truly needed another right-sided midfield player, bearing in mind that both Jason Price and Stuart Roberts were providing most of the existing attacking threat from that very position. Meanwhile, the glaring gaps on the left and in the centre of midfield were left unfilled.

An unlikely victory at Stoke's Britannia Stadium briefly raised hopes, but the team now needed to hit promotion form if they were to survive, and could never put such a run together. Relegation had become a formality, and was confirmed a week after Easter when Oldham won 2-1 at the Vetch. While the subsequent 6-0 hammering of Brentford at least gave the die-hard fans something to cheer, Hollins' post-match euphoria appeared wholly out of context. The manager appeared oblivious that the victory was achieved in a meaningless match, and that his team had been relegated with four matches to go. It wasn't even a close run thing.

The season had a final disappointing post-script, as Wrexham won 2-0 at The Vetch to claim the FAW Trophy. It was a particularly disappointing farewell for Giovanni Savarese, who was sent off after a few minutes. Savo had provided some much needed goal-power, although whether he was truly suited to the physical nature of the British game was debateable. Indeed, the game was chiefly memorable for the after match furore surrounding some rather chauvinistic comments made by BBC Wales analyst Mark Aizlewood regarding foreign players.

As the fall-out from a miserable season settled, Ninth Floor confirmed what many had suspected when it was announced that the club was once again up for sale. In truth, it did not look a particularly attractive proposition. An uncertain future loomed as the club faced life back in the Third Division after only one season, while a manager in whom most supporters had lost all faith continued *in situ*. The playing staff looked patchy, and there seemed every chance that the more promising members might be lost. Matters were exacerbated as the Swans once again passed Cardiff City in the opposite direction, and for the time being they appeared to be on an upward trajectory that contrasted with our own club's uncertain future.

Who would want to take over a struggling freshly relegated team who had a manager and number of players on lengthy and lucrative contracts, where the ground was a relic, and support ebbing away? The answer plumbed new depths even by the standards of a club that had been involved in the farces involving Michael Thompson, Kevin Cullis and Micky Adams.

*   *   *

With the confirmation that the club was now up for sale, the end of the Silver Shield – Ninth Floor era was in sight. If the Doug Sharpe era could be summed up in the word 'frustrating', then the single word that surely characterised the Swans' corporate phase was 'disappointing'. For all that might be said about Doug Sharpe, one could hardly accuse him of raising false expectations. In contrast, the statements made at the time of the Silver Shield takeover had led many Swans' fans to believe that better times were on the way. Whilst it should be said that the statements of ambition were strewn with caveats, the talk of Premiership potential and £50m stadium developments had inevitably inflated hopes.

However the reality had proved rather more prosaic. The board never invested the sums hoped for on the playing staff, and whilst this might have been justified when John Hollins led the club to promotion, the team were clearly in need of strengthening if they were to have retained their newly elevated status. Meanwhile the ambitious stadium project stalled. If these factors weren't bad enough, the board had alienated many supporters. The sacking of the popular Molby did not get matters off on the right footing, whilst the Micky Adams debacle left the new owners with a major credibility problem that was never properly redeemed despite a certain amount of success under Hollins.

By the time that the company by then known as Ninth Floor took their leave it was difficult for the outsider to see what – other than the creation of an infamous mascot - had been achieved. The team were back where they started in the Third Division. The club were solvent for the moment in so much that Ninth Floor had discharged existing liabilities and left £200,000 to cover short term running costs. Whilst it could be argued that this was not ungenerous, the problem was that once this money ran out that the club had ongoing liabilities that were highly problematic. There seemed few keen prospective purchasers waiting in the wings.

Certainly if viewed as a pure and simple business proposition, Swansea City football club looked a poor bet. Who would want to invest money in a club that was reportedly losing money on a regular basis? Indeed, one wonders if it was ever otherwise. However, the Silver Shield – Ninth Floor era represented a trend in British club ownership that became prevalent in late nineties Britain – the public limited company that sought to run a football club as a profit making concern.

Not that there was anything novel about football clubs having corporate status. Most clubs had been run as non-publicly quoted limited liability companies. As long as these companies remained small and didn't seek public investment they were by and large only answerable to their restricted membership of directors and shareholders. Further, there is nothing inherently wrong with attempting to run a football club at a profit rather than as a perennial loss leader. However, the new wave of corporate involvement that spread over the British game in the 1990s differed from its historic antecedents in ways that made many supporters come to question it's suitability as a device for running clubs.

Firstly the FA's restrictions on directors making personal profits out of clubs had been circumvented by the use of holding companies and corporate groups, rendering them obsolete for all practical purposes. Further, clubs began to seek public investment by flotation on the various financial markets. While this did enable clubs to raise additional funding that was on the face of it attractive, the primary duty of directors was now to the shareholders, in whose best interests the directors were required to act. There seemed ample scope for a conflict of interests between shareholders' financial well-being and the desires of supporters.

Many people were amazed that corporations, lenders and profit seeking investors ever saw football as ripe for rich pickings in the first place. While a few clubs such as Manchester United made a regular profit, most lived in a strange financial parallel reality. Doug Sharpe had reported that Swansea City had made losses even in relatively successful seasons. Even allowing for the alleged 'discipline' of the marketplace, on historical evidence it was hard to see many clubs turning things around.

However, two trends turned financiers' heads and made them reevaluate the football business. The first was the sudden media explosion, with television in particular paying escalating fees to screen matches. Add in the benefits of merchandising, and the intellectual property rights associated with a football club suddenly appeared very lucrative. Yet more sombre observers saw the inflated sums being paid to cover even lower division matches and asked how big this bubble could get.

Certainly the Swans seemed an unlikely starting point for a lucrative media empire, although the more optimistic fans would have argued that it had a large potential fan-base to draw upon. The difficulty was that for Swansea City's commercial potential to be realised there would have to be a fairly swift rise up the divisions, and realistically this would involve investment in the team. Had Swansea been the only club with ambitions then this would still have been far from a foregone conclusion, but with football's commercial boom it was obvious that there were other clubs out there talking the talk. If all these other ambitious clubs also started to throw money around then the seeds were being sown for rampant wage inflation that might make pre-war Germany appear stable.

In any event, success cannot always be bought on a football field, and it seemed a brave or foolish man who would gamble all on future business plans that could be upset by the vagaries of referees' decisions or the thickness of a post. Rather like share prices, football clubs can go up or down. It is difficult to credit that experienced businessmen, particularly in the case of Ninth Floor who had already run a successful venture, would not have accounted for these risks. Yet if the business schemes appeared highly optimistic with hindsight, it should be remembered that this was the era of the dot.com bubble, when financial rhyme and reason were apparently rendered redundant. In fact Ninth Floor got out before the bubble finally burst when the highly lucrative but optimistic ITV Digital television deal fell apart, although this was to be of little comfort to the Swans.

Alternatively, it may have been that Ninth Floor always regarded football as a long shot in terms of profit, and that their real interest was in the development of the new Morfa complex. Certainly property development was the other great nirvana that attracted investors to football. It seemed there were potential rich pickings in building a new stadium and developing retail and leisure facilities. Presumably Ninth Floor believed they could make a better fist of putting a feasible plan before the Council and raising the necessary capital than their predecessor. Ninth Floor had proposed a grand scheme for relocating during the 1997-98 season that had caused some initial excitement, but ultimately had got little further than most of the previous proposals.

The company blamed Swansea Council, but whether this was justifiable is debatable. The Council clearly had a remit that extended far beyond the football club. They had a duty to consider whether the detailed plans were right for the City as a whole. Local authorities can sometimes be soft targets if one wishes to divert flak, particularly if they can be portrayed as bureaucratic monoliths standing in the way of thrusting entrepreneurs. Whether this is fair depends on individual circumstances, but it should be remembered that Councils do not exist to be mere doormats for the grand schemes of property developers. For whatever reason, the Council didn't endorse the schemes put before them at that stage. The speed with which the Council later agreed terms for the development of the stadium with the new local ownership of the club says much in this regard. As the directors of Ninth Floor were unable to win hearts and minds amongst supporters, then perhaps it is unsurprising that they didn't enjoy any more success with Council members and officers.

Yet while the Ninth Floor regime may not have endeared themselves to supporters, one wonders whether the entire episode merely showed that the treatment of a club like Swansea City purely and simply as a profit generating business was conceptually flawed. The board had apparently attempted to modernise the club off the pitch, but in so doing had taken on a number of staff at rumoured high salaries. Meanwhile, player wages had gone through the roof, leaving many clubs with unsustainable overheads. One by one, a queue of Nationwide League clubs formed at administrators' offices around the country as the chickens let loose by the late 1990s wage explosion came home to roost. Very simply, the predicted boom of football media revenues failed to materialise for all but a few clubs, and those who had spent money in anticipation of future income were in deep trouble. Rather bigger fish than Swansea City fell into these particular choppy waters.

While those of us who watched from the sidelines as John Hollins' team was out-gunned might have cursed with frustration, there is an argument that matters could have been far worse if Ninth Floor had shown some of the 'ambition' demanded by fans. One of Ninth Floor's legacies that caused future problems were the contracts negotiated with players at the height of the market, the most high profile being Matthew Bound. However, these were the market rates at the time and most fans were vociferous in their calls for Bound to be re-signed. One can only imagine how much worse the position might have been if Ninth Floor had signed even more expensive players in anticipation of future revenues that never materialised.

Ultimately, the Ninth Floor era has to be judged a failure. However, it can be argued that Ninth Floor were part of a broader movement within British football at the time who believed that a club could be made into a profit making concern. The reality generally proved very different. Yet if supporters wanted the alleged benefits of the corporate world, such as the potentially huge sums of money that could be generated through flotation, they had also to accept the downside, in that the duty of public companies was to shareholders and not to either fans or broader community interests. If this was not always welcome news, then it was fundamentally related to the concept of football club as profit making corporate entity. If supporters didn't like it, they were going to have to find an alternative means of ownership structure and financing.

Meanwhile, the fans were going to have to deal with someone with a very different concept of the club as profit making machine.

Nick Cusack and Trevor Watkins of Supporters Direct
at the public meeting in 2001
(Photo: Supporters Trust)

Supporters march in Swansea's Oxford Street October 2001
(Photo: Supporters Trust)

12. Rage against the dying of the white

As the storm clouds gathered on the horizon during the summer months of 2001, Swansea City fans began attempting to ensure the continued survival of the club. The route ahead had been uncertain since the 'For Sale' signs had gone up, and few supporters were under any illusion that there was to be a fast and positive solution. Many realised that the very existence of the club was in the balance, and that if the Swans were to have a future, somebody somewhere had to do something. With little interest being shown by potential new owners, many fans began to realise that it was time to act. Too often in recent years they had been forced to sit watching from the sidelines, having no voice to air concerns and grievances. Many supporters wanted to ensure that not only would the club survive but that this time around they would actually have a role in future decision taking.

The growth of fan power was a relatively recent phenomenon. In the past, the Swans had possessed supporters' organisations that had played an active role in fund raising, but had never sought any more influential role. The traditional old-fashioned supporters' club was largely a passive animal from a more deferential age. In days when ordinary folk 'knew their place', organisations at some clubs were grateful if they even received thanks for their efforts.

Yet these associations played an important part in raising money for their clubs. At Swansea, for instance, the supporters had raised around £16,000 in the late 1950s for the building of the roof over the North Bank, and later contributed to the cost of installing floodlights. The irony was that this money was handed over at a time when crowds were large, the end of the maximum wage was only just in sight, and a potentially great team was being sold off. If there were mutterings in the town as to where the money was going, the ordinary supporter was not to be privy to such information. If they wanted the comfort of a roof over their heads, they had to pay for it themselves.

Even in the crisis winter of 1985, when society was generally less reverential, supporters gathered funds through the SOS (Save Our Swans) appeal and handed them over to the club with little expectation that this would entitle them to anything other than a pat on the back. Local business adviser Roger Warren Evans was featured in the *Evening Post* suggesting some form of community ownership, an idea that meant little in Britain, but was not unusual in Europe. However, the idea was given little serious consideration. Instead, the money was effectively passed on to help ensure the survival of the club, and whilst that may have been satisfying to many who contributed, there was no reward in terms of a seat at the decision makers table.

Gradually, however, the attitude of football supporters around Britain was hardening. The disasters at Bradford and Hillsborough served to highlight what many people had suspected for years – that the organisation of events by the authorities was not all it should be. Club administrators, the football authorities and police no longer had the trust of vast swathes of the paying public. Many supporters were presenting a more thoughtful and coherent aspect of the football fan in contrast to the lurid image portrayed in some sections of the media. Questions were now being raised in an intelligent manner regarding various aspects of the way the game was being run.

In particular, financial affairs at many clubs were being called into question. The phenomenon of the asset-stripper was not unknown at football clubs in the 1980s and several found that their traditional home grounds were attractive to property speculators. Wolves and Chelsea found themselves skating on thin ice in this regard, while more complex circumstances led to Charlton losing their home. Many clubs' fans formed independent supporters associations as pressure or lobby groups to highlight and publicise what they believed were disreputable dealings at their clubs. The national Football Supporters Association formed an umbrella organisation to co-ordinate efforts when interests ran parallel.

As the football world began to change in the 1990s, such organisations took on a higher profile. The targets of campaigns included Brighton chairman Derek Archer, whose consortium left Brighton homeless by selling the Goldstone Ground with no replacement in sight. The 'Fans United' movement at Brighton may not have won that particular battle, but it did provide a focus that helped the Seagulls survive, despite a two-year exile in Gillingham. As mentioned in a previous chapter, Charlton fans had provided much of the inspiration for such movements, their 'Back to the Valley' campaign breathing life and energy into a club that was on its last legs, and paving the way for success based on a solid relationship between fans and the new board. On a very different scale, Manchester United's organised grouping of small shareholders fought a proposed takeover by Rupert Murdoch, one of the most powerful men in the world, and won.

The medium through which the early campaigns were often co-ordinated were the fanzines. Developed from the photocopy and staple precedent of punk rock culture, the football fanzine became the soap-box enabling fans to express their views. Tired of the bland outpourings of the official club programmes with their clichés and stereotypes, the fanzines offered an alternative voice. Often intelligent, sometimes abusive, rarely boring, their quality varied greatly. All provided a voice for supporters independent of the official line.

In truth, coherent fan activism had largely passed Swansea City by during the early to mid-1990s. Aside from a few spontaneous demonstrations against Doug Sharpe following poor performances on the pitch, there had been little formal articulation of supporter concern. There was no independent supporters association to challenge the powers that be in an effective manner, while the state of fanzines had been patchy.

None had hung around long enough to become the established alternative voice of Swansea fans. Much more effective were supporters' internet sites, including Gary Martin's unofficial Swansea City site that emerged in the mid-1990s to pose awkward questions to the Ninth Floor regime.

As the financial landscape of football changed in the 1990s, fans across Britain decided to take their criticism of the way that their clubs were being managed a step further. Almost invariably these developments were precipitated by crises. Bournemouth appeared to be the latest in the line of clubs to face the genuine possibility of extinction early in the decade, but the fans decided enough was enough, and by effectively co-ordinating the supporters' various talents, the club was saved thanks to the setting up of a trust. Similar events occurred at Lincoln and Chesterfield. These clubs were not only saved from extinction, but were now owned and administered by genuine supporters with no other agenda than giving their clubs a viable future. For those who believed that this was the manifestation of some hitherto undiscovered left wing insurrection, the trusts contained members from a wide variety of backgrounds, and from across the political spectrum. This was not about politics in a narrow party sense, but about the broader politics of people caring what happened in their community, and attempting to protect its facilities from those who threatened them.

Many of the developments in football since the inception of the Premiership had worried the all-party parliamentary football committee, and the Football Task Force was set up following the 1997 General Election to address some of the issues. Predictably, the various powerful interest groups lobbied hard, and the impact of that body's recommendations became diluted. The more radical suggestions for keeping football clubs' roots firmly in their communities and the moneymen in check were kicked to touch. However, one of the more positive aspects that survived was the development of Supporters Direct, a government body specifically set up to assist supporters establish trusts to safeguard the long term existence of clubs.

While there were cynics who dismissed the trust concept as 'rule by committee', logic suggested that any collection of supporters would possess a wide variety of talents. Across the country, many club owners had shown themselves to be in various degrees dishonest, irresponsible, unrealistic, unimaginative, overly conservative or incompetent. Surely the pooling of the diverse talents present in the supporter body could not do any worse?

Not that we should have needed reminding of the power of collective action in South Wales. The area was, after all, at the forefront of the organised labour, co-operative and mutual movements that helped transform the lives of the majority of ordinary people for the better, by standing up against more powerful forces. If such activities were seen as from a different age, then more recent precedents had been set in Wales. Both the successful tourist steam railways of the North, and nearby Tower

Colliery had shown that businesses dismissed as basket-cases by so-called experts could be run viably where the motivation was not purely for excessive profit. People united in purpose can achieve a huge amount.

By the end of the disastrous 2000-01 season, a group of Swansea fans could see the writing on the wall at the Vetch, and rather than sit crying into their pint glasses, decided to try to do something about it. An initial public meeting was held at the Brangwyn Hall in May 2001, and interest was sufficient for the project to get off the ground. As events at the club evolved as the summer wore on, concern amongst supporters became even greater. A first open meeting was held at the Patti Pavilion following the Cheltenham game in August, and with membership numbers growing as the crisis at the club deepened, the ball was very firmly rolling. Whatever the eventual outcome might be, Swansea fans were not going to allow the club to either die without a fight.

They needed to be prepared, because history was to show that the football authorities would do little to assist. We had known that many owners did not necessarily have the best interests of their clubs at heart. However, many fans were genuinely shocked at the apparent indifference of football's ruling bodies to the manner in which the games traditions and heritage were being distorted and destroyed.

Previous owners had not supplied the answers to the conundrum that was Swansea City. Credible new owners were not exactly clamouring at the gates of the Vetch Field, and it seemed unlikely that the football authorities would be of much assistance. Swansea supporters faced the stark reality that nobody from the outside was likely to help. If the club was to have a future, they were going to have to do things for themselves.

*　　　*　　　*

Swansea City played out two seasons during 2001-02. One involved an evolving drama that after numerous twists to the plot was to eventually provide a happy ending. Somewhere alongside, a little football was played which occasionally stole the headlines from the off-field saga.

The first major development over the summer was the long anticipated exit of Ninth Floor. However, the circumstances of their departure were hardly ideal. The club had been transferred to former commercial director Mike Lewis for the princely sum of £1. Lewis had become reviled by many supporters as epitomising the problems of the club, receiving what was rumoured to be an inflated salary while fans remained unconvinced of his worth. If the fee for which the club changed hands was the subject of derision in some quarters, the more sombre reality was that the club was now staring disaster in the face. Ninth Floor had cleared the overdraft, discharged the club's immediate debts and left £200,000 to tide the club through the early weeks of the season, but beyond that it was difficult to see who would continue to subsidise it.

Lewis was ostensibly owner on an interim basis while he sought fresh investment, but few believed that he had the personal resources to keep the club going once the Ninth Floor money ran out. Swansea City was sitting on a time bomb and the clock was ticking.

The summer had seen an exodus of players who were out of contract. Predictably, Walter Boyd and Giovanni Savarese had left, the latter being taken on trial by Millwall. Fabiano and Verchave had returned to France, although compatriot David Romo remained. Jason Price left for an extended trial at Brentford before eventually joining Tranmere, while Steve Jones had rejoined Cheltenham. Martin Thomas had left for Brighton before the previous season's transfer deadline, although his subsequent career vindicated those that felt that he had never wholly recovered from the injury sustained against West Ham.

Strangely, two people who might well have been expected to leave remained as the new season began, although neither was to last the season. Stuart Roberts had been the subject of much transfer speculation, being the club's most saleable youngster, but only Rotherham made a definite move. Stuart spent a week on trial in South Yorkshire, but returned to the Vetch stating that he felt that the Swans were a naturally bigger club. The young winger's comments were typical of the attitude that endeared him to fans, but with hindsight perhaps both his club and international career would have developed more positively had he joined the First Division club.

Meanwhile, John Hollins also survived in the manager's chair, although few fans had confidence in his ability to turn things around. Supporters had become almost sanguine about his presence, for it seemed that if he wasn't sacked following the disasters of the previous season then he never would be. Possibly Lewis was still confident at that point of selling the club on quickly, leaving the new owners to resolve the managerial situation with its attendant awkward issue of compensation. Hollins was even allowed to sign players, John Williams returning to the club where he had started his professional career. Argentine midfield player Nicolas Messina was signed after impressing in pre-season matches, while Mamade Sidibe, a Malian born striker from France who had also impressed during trials was handed a year's contract.

The pre-season programme included a match against the Jamaican national team. While there was disappointment that Walter Boyd did not appear, the Reggae Boyz entertained the crowd with a free-flowing display in the sunshine that was a pleasant contrast to the more basic qualities that we were likely to witness in the Third Division. Sadly, the game didn't attract the support that such an exotic fixture deserved, partly due to the pricing policy adopted.

When the season finally got underway, the team won spectacularly at Macclesfield on the opening day, with Sidibe getting on the score sheet in a 3-1 success. For at least a week die-hard fans dreamed that the club could succeed on the pitch despite the off-field troubles. However, a goalless draw at home to Oxford brought a touch of reality to proceedings, while a 3-0 defeat at Lincoln suggested that the season ahead could be tough going.

Hollins remained in charge until after a 3-1 reverse at early leaders Plymouth. It was rumoured that the decision to sack him had actually been taken before the previous match, a 4-2 home win over Exeter. This just increased the feeling that while the dismissal was hardly a surprise, the timing was strange. Surely the logical thing was to have made the change over the summer, allowing a new man the chance to bring players in. Perhaps there had been no time due to the change of ownership, but to sack Hollins six games into the new season merely added to the feeling of confusion surrounding the club.

Colin Addison was to be the new manager with Peter Nicholas as his assistant. Interestingly, Addison had been in the frame for the Swansea job before John Toshack was appointed. He was probably a good choice given the difficult circumstances, having wide experience at a variety of levels in the game from Merthyr Tydfil to Atletico Madrid. The latter job had brought him into contact with the colourful Jesus Gil, a man with a reputation for disposing of managers almost as fast as Swansea City. However, if Addo thought he had seen it all, fate still had some new tricks up its sleeve. His experience of working under difficult conditions was certainly to come in useful.

Addison began unspectacularly, but results gradually improved and the team held a place in lower mid table throughout most of this spell. In need of a full back to effectively replace Steve Jones, Addison recruited Terry Evans, a former Cardiff trainee who had been playing at Barry. Nathan Tyson arrived on loan from Reading, and while hardly a household name, added pace to an attack that by now was missing Sidibe, who had picked up the first in a series of injuries. Addison saw the side record its first win under his control over Jan Molby's Kidderminster in September, and suddenly there seemed a little light at the end of the tunnel.

At this stage it had been easy for supporters to hide their heads in the sand as to the financial position, but with Ninth Floor's money about to run out and gates disappointing, something had to give. When the change came, it was devastating. The news emerged in the first few days of October that the club had been sold to Tony Petty, an Australian businessman with roots in South London. Petty had a background in Australian soccer, but as rumours spread over the internet, concern grew. It was less than clear how he was going to bankroll a club that was in a critical state financially.

Having watched his first match, a 1-0 defeat at home to a high-flying Rochdale side, Petty made the move that was to give him his infamous place in the history of Swansea City. On Thursday 11 October it was announced that almost the entire first team squad were to be sacked by the club. While nobody pretended that many of the players involved were world-beaters, they were solid professionals who constituted the backbone of the side, and without their presence it was difficult to see that the club could compete in the Third Division. Many supporters now believed that this was the act of a man who lacked football sense, legal knowledge, moral scruples and public relations skills. If anybody had previously been in any doubt, it was now crystal clear – Swansea City were in a crisis that could prove terminal. The fate of Newport County beckoned, and Swansea fans woke up at night in cold sweats.

At this point, Nick Cusack seized the moment to emerge as a leader of the players, and to secure his own place in the folklore of Swansea City. As Professional Footballers Association representative, he rallied his men, and quickly sought the union's advice. Petty had foolishly placed himself not only with a moral and public relations mountain to climb, but also in an untenable legal position. Realising his mistake he subsequently attempted to backtrack, but his true colours had now been revealed.

Quite what motivated Petty was hard to judge. There was no freehold property interest in the ground for the club owner to exploit, and if the Council would not advance the Morfa project with Ninth Floor, it was hardly likely to deal with Petty following the furore over his actions. The popular theory was that he sought to exploit what few assets the club had left. Certainly Stuart Roberts, the club's most saleable player, was soon on his way to Wycombe Wanderers for a fee of £100,000, a disappointing destination and fee for a player of much promise. If Sidibe's fitness had not been an issue he would almost certainly have also been sold over the next few weeks. It certainly seems unlikely that Petty ever had any credible long-term plan for the club.

The team, sacked or not, played at Southend and the fans should always remember the debt owed to the squad who turned up and played that day. The performance in a 4-2 defeat was more spirited than anybody could have expected. Stuart Roberts, playing on a week-to-week contract, was rumoured to have turned out unpaid. Stuart emotionally celebrated a consolation goal in front of the away support in what everybody realised was surely a farewell performance. Whatever else, Petty's intervention appeared to have galvanised the spirit of both the fans and the team. The fight against injustice was on.

The fans rallied around the team's efforts, and the Supporters Trust became the focal point. Meanwhile, the internet sites provided a stream of up-to-date information ensuring that supporters were kept abreast of Petty's every move. In particular, Phil Sumbler's *JackArmy* site enjoyed its finest hour, apparently possessing sources within the club beyond the reach of many established journalists. If the information superhighway kept fans aware of the latest developments, the old fashioned highway provided a venue for protest. A march from Castle Square to The Vetch, joined by fans of other clubs prefaced the home match against Leyton Orient. At the ground, the Orient fans endeared themselves to the Swansea faithful by unveiling a banner in support of the cause.

When a public meeting was organised at the Patti Pavilion, the team attended alongside the fans and Nick Cusack spoke like a true leader. Out of adversity was emerging strength. The fixture against Rushden in November was attended by Petty and was remarkable for the unrelenting atmosphere of hatred directed at one individual. The match itself seemed almost incidental.

Through all this, the players had to somehow continue playing football. Almost inevitably, results were patchy, but enough points were being won to keep the team out of the relegation fight. Despite the off-field distractions, the team produced one of its finest performances for several seasons when disposing of QPR from the FA Cup in front of Sky Television's cameras. The 4-0 win featured a magnificent performance from Sidibe, who then became the latest subject of transfer speculation. The television fee probably helped prolong the Petty era, for it was arguable that had the club gone out of the cup at the first hurdle in a non-televised match, matters may have been brought to a head earlier.

The week of the QPR match proved to be a false dawn for the Swans faithful, the fine cup victory prefacing a solid 2-0 win at York that suggested matters might be picking up in the league. More importantly, former player and director Mel Nurse had embarked on legal action against Petty with a view to forcing him out. However, the outcome of the court hearing on 28 November was a disappointment, the case being adjourned, leaving Petty to fight another day. To compound the disappointment of a black Friday, the team lost 1-0 at home to Hartlepool in the evening.

Throughout this period Mike Lewis refused to disappear, popping up in unexpected places like the proverbial scarlet pimpernel. Lewis had never exactly been a man of the people, but now, in many supporters' eyes he had become the second most hated man in Swansea. With an astonishing lack of social awareness, he even attempted to drink in the Harry Griffiths Bar following the theatre of hate of the Rushden match, causing a predictable furore. To compound matters, Lewis was subsequently quoted in the local press questioning whether the sale had been legitimately completed. To put matters politely, Lewis's role in matters was bemusing.

If the four goals in the FA Cup against QPR had handed Petty a financial lifeline, Macclesfield scored four in 10 minutes in the next round to put paid to any hopes the owner may have had of a major cash bonanza. If this result ironically raised hopes that the Petty era might come to an early close, there was cold comfort for the players. In a tale that might have been written by Charles Dickens, the players were not paid on time just days before Christmas. It was arguable that they could have legally walked away at that point, but commendably they not only turned up at Exeter on Boxing Day, but produced one of the performances of the season in a 3-0 win.

By this stage the team was regularly featuring three players Addison had plucked from outside the Football League, Terry Evans having been joined by Scarborough's Steve Brodie and Merthyr's Neil Sharpe. Sharpe had apparently longed for an opportunity in the professional game. Whether he was achieving that by playing for a team that didn't get paid is an interesting philosophical point. Petty had allegedly been relying on the investment of a mystery benefactor who bore the unlikely name of Mrs Duck. That these claims sounded decidedly Mickey Mouse was confirmed when the alleged golden egg never appeared. There was probably more chance of Cyril the Swan laying one.

By January the game was up for Petty, and it was announced that he was open to offers for the club. Rumours abounded of Mel Griffin, a London based property developer buying the club. However, after all the upheavals and broken promises of the recent past, most fans were relieved when it was announced that a local consortium would step in, with a major stake being held by the Supporters' Trust. At this stage the most important thing seemed to be to put the club back in the hands of those who genuinely cared for it. However, the new board warned that the club remained in deep trouble. Some supporters believed that ridding the club of Petty represented victory. However, while an important battle had been won, the war had still to run its course, and the tale had twists yet to come.

Meanwhile, a decent run of form saw the club climb the table during February, and three successive wins effectively saw off the threat of relegation. However, shock waves again reverberated from Glamorgan Terrace when Addison and Nicholas were dismissed. It seems the new administration were concerned to resolve the financial problems, and acted as soon as the team appeared to be safe from relegation. Whilst fans had to trust the new board's financial judgement, there were those who felt that the club had acted hastily. If there were tough days ahead then many believed Addison's experience should not have been discarded.

Nick Cusack and Roger Freestone were placed in charge as a joint caretaker team, and in many respects were popular choices. Cusack was clearly an intelligent individual, and his role in the black days of the previous winter had established his leadership qualities. The new pairing enjoyed a reasonable start by beating promotion candidates Mansfield in a fine performance notable for a spectacular goal by David Romo, something of a forgotten man. However, reality soon set in, and defeats by 7-1 at Hartlepool and 4-0 at Rushden were ominous. Failure to record a further win saw the side subside to a 20th place finish.

By the end, most people were just glad that the season was over and that the club had lived to fight another day. The football had too often become a sideshow to the off-field soap opera. It was obvious that radical changes were necessary on the pitch. There would clearly be many departures over the summer to join Richie Appleby and Nicolas Messina who had already been released by Addison. The main interest surrounded who would take over the manager's chair and make those decisions. Little did we realise that the next instalment of the Swansea City story would feature a drama on the pitch any bit as gripping as the saga that had evolved over the previous winter.

Off the field, matters were stabilised as the club announced that it was entering a Company Voluntary Arrangement. Inevitably, there would be people hurt financially in the process, but it was difficult to see any alternative. To have attempted to trade out of the inherited financial mess would have been at best difficult and at worst criminal. The proposals were carried, giving the club some breathing space, but the next two years were clearly going to be tough, as a tight ship would have to be run for the club to stay afloat.

Perhaps the overwhelming experience of the season, however, was a sense of the community coming together to claim back one of its institutions. From now on Swansea fans would be keeping a careful eye on prospective owners of the club, and the importance of scrutiny and openness in dealings was paramount. The season had shown the potential dangers when one man has sole control of a football club with no outside agents to act as checks and balances. Among the fans there was widespread support for the concept of shared ownership with the trust gaining a seat on the board with a view to playing a substantial role in rebuilding the club along community lines. The idea of broader based club ownership, well established in Europe, was growing quietly but steadily across Britain. For once, Swansea City appeared to be at the forefront of a new development in British football that might not have been loudly heralded in the media, but which in the long term might come to have a significant influence on the way the game is run.

*   *   *

Yet again, the season 2001-02 had seen managerial musical chairs at the Vetch Field. For the second time in four years the club went through three managerial teams in a season. Looking for silver linings, at least matters never got as chaotic as in 1995-96.

The season had commenced with John Hollins in charge. If at other times the club could be justly criticised for lack of managerial stability, on this occasion many thought a change overdue. Yet the timing of his dismissal appeared strange, as many fans believed he would have departed over the close season following relegation. One suspects that a combination of instability in the boardroom and the practical constraints of finance kept him in a job. Ironically, the team's form at the time the axe fell did not represent a particularly dreadful start.

How then, to assess Hollins period in charge? This is one of the most difficult questions of the entire period covered by this book. Hollins first two seasons were respectively good and exceptional in terms of final league position. While the third was dreadful, the strange aspect was that many fans had turned against the manager while the good times were still rolling. Why was a man who had delivered a first championship in 48 years so reviled by certain sections of the support?

Perhaps the main difficulty surrounded the style of football that earned the success. Rightly or wrongly, Swansea fans believe their team should play with a certain panache. While the likes of Wimbledon or Sheffield United might believe that ends justify any means, other teams demand not only success, but success with style. Rather like West Ham, Swansea City's history weighs heavily on the type of football expected by fans.

It seemed that Hollins did initially encourage a ground based passing game. However, he was bequeathed a team built largely by Alan Cork, who had a rather more basic vision of the way to achieve success in the lower divisions. For all Hollins' early principles, results improved when a more basic direct style was employed. The long high ball aimed toward Julian Allsop reaped rewards, and once established, the pattern proved difficult to throw off. Could Hollins really be blamed for keeping with a tactic that suited the players at his disposal and was successful?

Strangely, during the disastrous relegation season, it appeared that Hollins recognised that more flair was needed in the team, and he recruited the likes of Romo and Fabiano who were undoubtedly skilful players. Yet the team as a whole appeared ill-equipped to play such a style. Might the season have evolved differently if Hollins had stuck to the methodical approach that had served him well? Did the 5-1 reverse at Reading affect not only the team's confidence, but also the manager's self belief? Some supporters believed he might have done better to have retained the organised style but recruited a slightly better class of player to execute it.

However, supporters' reservations about Hollins were not limited to events on the pitch. Perhaps part of his problem was his presentational style. If Molby and Adams had been slick communicators, and Cork somewhat diffident, Hollins was simply bemusing. Supporters frequently scratched their heads as they attempted to make sense of his musings. Yet this could surely not be the deeper reason for the antipathy among fans. After all, Frankie Burrows was not necessarily the slickest of interviewees, yet he never suffered similar criticism.

A far more serious charge laid by some supporters was that Hollins never acknowledged the weaknesses in the team, and he was viewed in some quarters as little more than an apologist for the transfer policies of the board. In fairness, he may have been informed of the lack of funds available for team building before he was appointed, and did not think it appropriate to complain after accepting the job. Further, he may have believed that to have played to the gallery and publicly criticised players by stating that some were not good enough would have been counter-productive and undermined morale. While these are reasonable arguments, the counter is that there comes a point where to maintain that a team is good enough with a record of one win in 22 matches must surely have led the players to doubt whether the manager had a handle on reality. To maintain hopeless optimism in the face of damning statistics must surely lead to a loss of credibility in the dressing room.

Ultimately, a manager is assessed on results, and Hollins record speaks for itself. Few could quibble with the bare statistics of his first two seasons in charge. A cup run and play off spot had been followed with promotion and a championship. Bearing in mind that this was essentially the same team that had finished in twentieth place the season before he took over, and outsiders might think that his critics were being a little churlish. Added to that, the team created club records for both successive league wins and clean sheets, while boasting the best defensive record in the Nationwide League. However, the relegation season was a disaster to which Hollins appeared to have no real answers. The failure to strengthen may not necessarily have been his fault, but certain lapses in judgement almost certainly were. Perhaps John Hollins erred by not quitting while he was marginally still ahead, in which case perhaps his period in charge would be seen by many supporters in a better light with hindsight than at the time.

Colin Addison was probably a good choice to take over from Hollins, in that he had a reputation as something of a trouble-shooter. Older fans would also have remembered Addison's success in turning ailing Newport County around in the 1970s. It was to Addison's eternal credit that he managed to keep the Swans out of the relegation fight despite the horrendous off-field distractions. The team played to a recognisable and well-balanced shape, and Addison seemed to both get the best out of the players available, playing a system suited to their strengths and weaknesses. He certainly appeared to get the best out of Andrew Mumford whose career plummeted after he left. Again, he obviously knew the non-league scene well, and supplemented his squad with players drawn from the semi-professional ranks who performed a valuable job.

One can only speculate what might have happened had the Addison-Nicholas partnership been allowed to both see out the season and build for the future. Many supporters believed that the club would not have gone through the traumas of the following season had Addison remained in charge. Ultimately, it seems that finance was the cause of the management downfall rather than any specific complaint on the pitch. The precise details never became public, but supporters had to trust the new board that the decision was in the longer-term interests of the club. Yet the general view on the terraces was that Addison was treated poorly, and had done much to preserve the club's league status when things could otherwise have fallen apart. Perhaps the era is best remembered on the pitch for the hammering of QPR that provided something heart lifting for the faithful when all else was looking incredibly bleak.

Nick Cusack became the third manager employed by the Swans that season. While theoretically the caretaker role was jointly held with Roger Freestone, Cusack was perceived by most as the senior partner due to his role in leading the players through the Petty mess. This view was confirmed when Cusack was appointed full-time in his own right the following summer. Cusack the player had not been universally popular with the fans, as his unspectacular style often went unappreciated, while his staunch defence of John Hollins didn't endear him to some sections of the support. However, his role in opposing Petty and in keeping team morale from falling apart elevated him to hero status.

Sadly, despite the promising start to Cusack's period in charge, the team slumped over the final five games of the season, and finished 20th, one of their lowest positions of the campaign. At the time most fans were too relieved that Petty had been seen off to worry overmuch about the precise position above the safety line the club finished. However, with hindsight perhaps we should already have seen the writing on the wall, particularly after the humiliations at Hartlepool and Rushden.

Nick Cusack was probably the wrong man in the wrong place at the wrong time. His subsequent wholesale changes to the playing squad didn't produce the required results, and when the club struggled from the outset the following season, the axe duly fell. Perhaps the board were asking too much of a man who had earned the adoration of the fans but possessed little hands–on management experience. The clubs' financial position suggested an old head in the Addison or Burrows mould was needed, and to expect a managerial novice to keep the club out of trouble at that stage was probably unrealistic. Eventually the board were forced to eat humble pie and acknowledge that a mistake had been made.

However, over the summer of 2002 most fans were content that the club had survived and would be kicking off the new season. Meanwhile the board allowed the new young manager to go about his work. If they thought they could expect a quiet life they were soon to be proved mistaken. Supporters were growing used to the fact that life with Swansea City was seldom dull.

Action at The Vetch: Nick Cusack in action against Hartlepool in 2002
(Photo: *South Wales Evening Post*)

James Thomas scoring a crucial penalty
against Hull City at The Vetch, May 2003
(Photo: Gary Martin)

Leon Britton (Photo: Andrew Thomas)

Roberto Martinez (Photo: Andrew Thomas)

Part Four: Redemption and rebirth

13. Crisis? What crisis?

For many Swansea City supporters, the summer of 2002 was once again a time of hope and anticipation. The club was back in local ownership after the disasters of previous regimes. The team was back in an all-white strip with black trim. There were new signings, including a local lad returning to boost his home-town team. Little did most supporters realise the trauma that still lay ahead. If the previous season had seen a close shave with death due to events in the boardroom, then this time around the drama was to be on the pitch.

There were potential rich pickings available that summer as around 800 professional players sought work as the result of the new wind of financial reality blowing through the Nationwide League in the wake of the collapse of the ITV Digital television deal. The Swans had themselves supplied a fair proportion as Cusack cleared the decks to make room to bring new players in. Jonathan Coates, Chris Todd, Ryan Casey, David Romo, Jason Jones and Steve Brodie were all released, while the club also relinquished the registration of Mamade Sidibe who had failed to return after the summer. Whilst one could understand Cusack's reluctance to deal with the agent of a player who didn't seem to want to play for the club, the loss of the big Malian was a blow, emphasised by his subsequent success at First Division Gillingham.

New arrivals included Bury pair Matt Murphy and Paul Reid, Dave Smith from Grimsby, Dave Theobald from Brentford, James Wood from Halifax and Dave Moss from Chesterfield. Chances were handed to Carmarthen's prolific young striker Jonathon Keaveney, and Pontardawe's former Liverpool trainee goalkeeper Mike Marsh. However, the signing that encouraged most genuine enthusiasm was that of former Swansea schoolboy James Thomas who had been released by Blackburn.

The opening fixture was played out before a large vociferous crowd on a sunny day at the Vetch Field against a team clad in yellow. If you squinted your eyes a little it was momentarily possible to believe that we had been miraculously transported back to 1981 and the glorious summers day when Leeds were put to the sword. Sadly, the illusion only lasted a few minutes before Rushden took a deserved lead. This time around, traditional pre-season optimism had been punctured within a quarter of an hour. Still the hard-core support tried to accentuate the positive, and post match talk centred around James Thomas's classic back post header to square things up, and Paul Reid's spectacular long range shot that briefly gave the Swans a 2-1 lead.

However, the sheer lateness of Rushden's equaliser couldn't entirely disguise the shortcomings, and supporters clung to the hope that the Swans would be unlikely to face as demanding opposition as the big spending Midlanders on a regular basis. Fans persuaded themselves that the team would be equipped to deal with the more mundane opposition likely to be faced from week to week. However, successive away defeats at less fancied Bury and Bristol Rovers put matters in perspective, and a dishevelled performance at Wrexham effectively brought Nick Cusack's stewardship to an end.

One could only speculate as to whether the tension of the months ahead might have been spared had an experienced manager been allowed to recruit his own squad during the close season. Instead, the job had been left to the inexperienced Nick Cusack, who gamely organised trial matches for those who were interested in coming to West Wales.

While Thomas started the season brightly and was to again come good when it mattered, the feeling began to grow that the new arrivals had done little to improve the overall strength of the squad, and indeed may even have weakened it. Defeat at Boston in Nick Cusack's final match sent the club to the bottom of the Football League for the first time ever. Sadly, it was not to be the last.

Bearing in mind the financial constraints of the Creditors Voluntary Arrangement that restricted the club, the employment of an experienced manager seemed sensible, and the appointment of Brian Flynn in late September was of little surprise. He might well have been appointed over the summer, but his insistence that Kevin Reeves accompany him as assistant proved a sticking point. Flynn was belatedly to have his way.

Flynn and Reeves had enjoyed longevity at Wrexham where the side were transformed from bottom of the old fourth division to upper mid-table in the new second, with a series of cup giant-killings to boot. Flynn had also enjoyed a degree of success in managing the Welsh under-21 team, and many people had felt he would have been a better choice to take over the senior national side than Bobby Gould. However, his final season with Wrexham had been something of a disaster, and he arrived at the Vetch with a reputation to retrieve.

Flynn certainly tightened the team's approach in the short term, and at least the comic book defending of the early games was rectified. From the start, he dispensed with the majority of Cusack's signings with the exception of James Thomas and Jamie Wood. However, while the side ground out a few results that raised hopes that the club could climb into mid-table, a dreadful 4-0 home defeat in October by what proved to be a rather ordinary Kidderminster side left nobody in any doubt that league status was under threat.

It was obvious that if relegation were to be averted, the squad required strengthening. Bright young hopefuls such as Alan Tate, Leon Britton and Marc Richards arrived on loan deals from Premiership clubs, but despite an encouraging win over Shrewsbury the storyboard remained on course for a depressing end. Some felt that while Flynn had boosted the squad with youth and natural ability, he was employing a 4-3-3 formation that was as outmoded as the Bump or Hustle in a modern night club. Meanwhile, players who had performed with promise in the past disappointed, with Andrew Mumford in particular a shadow of the

150

previous season's player of the year.

Six consecutive defeats around Christmas saw the team fall six points adrift at the bottom of the table by mid January, and many fans spent the gloomy evenings of the New Year disconsolately planning routes to places such as Leigh and Woking. Where exactly was Forest Green, anyway? Foreboding was in the air as winter's gloom deepened.

Bo Eklund, brother of Swedish actress Britt, expressed interest in taking the club over. However, the details of his plans were vague, while the approach itself was made in an unusual manner. Bearing in mind events at the club over the recent past, the majority of fans were nonplussed, and showed a rather less than enthusiastic response. In any event, Eklund lost interest following the lukewarm reception.

As January drew to a close the team were re-enforced by the recruitment of experienced heads in the shape of Kevin Nugent, Lenny Johnrose and Roberto Martinez. A good performance at league leaders Rushden in a 1-1 draw shown live on Sky Television followed a 2-0 win over Lincoln, and suddenly there was hope in the air. Gradually, the skies and mood were lightening as spring approached and survival suddenly seemed feasible. The team took on a more professional appearance, and the likes of Britton were clearly benefiting from the greater experience and competence around them. Martinez in particular was proving influential, organising the team and radiating a class and control in midfield that had arguably been missing from the team since the heyday of Cornforth or Molby. To make way for the new arrivals, several of Cusack's summer signings had their contracts paid up and left.

Not only did results begin to pick up, but the team were now playing in a style that the wider world might recognise as football. Yet every time it seemed they were about to pull clear of trouble, a new twist would take matters back a pace. A shocking refereeing decision in a crucial home fixture with Carlisle was only matched by an inept team performance in a 2-1 defeat. Two awful defeats over Easter, including a 1-0 home loss to rivals Exeter turned up the heat.

Luckily, Flynn tinkered with his resources at the last and setting aside his McCarthyesque aversion to left-wingers, played the recently re-signed Jonathan Coates in the two crucial final games. Over 1,000 Swans' fans made the trip to Rochdale for the final away fixture, virtually turning it into a home game. Again the team disregarded the heart conditions of their fans, surrendering an early lead before Marc Richards scored a late winner that agonisingly crept over the line off a post in what seemed like slow motion. Even then a scramble in the Swansea goalmouth in the last minute could have spelt disaster, but luckily the ball flew over the bar. Relief at a vital win was short lived, however, as news was confirmed that Exeter had secured an unlikely away victory, and the calculation became simple. Win at the Vetch in the final game against Hull, and Football League status was safe. Anything less, and we were dependent on Exeter slipping up.

The final day of the 2002-3 season will go down as one of the most dramatic in the history of Swansea City. It was a day as tense as any of the final day dramas from the Toshack era, but with added ingredient that the price of failure would be obscurity and humiliation. The word nervous is inadequate to describe the feeling in the build-up. The match was a sell out but the singing and noise level before the teams came out were not quite enough to blot out the voice of doubt that nagged and recalled the price if it all went wrong.

A James Thomas penalty gave the Swans an early lead, but Hull levelled almost immediately. A disastrous error gave Hull the lead, and suddenly the prospects seemed as grim as the unseasonable weather. The road to Margate loomed. Neil Cutler, a goalkeeper borrowed from Stoke City to deputise for the injured Roger Freestone, pulled off a magnificent save to stop Hull going further ahead. If the nerves had been jangling early on, they were now as taut as a guitar string.

Exeter were now being run by Mike Lewis, and for the Swansea faithful the thought of the man who they believed had done so much to damage the club coming out ahead added further frisson to affairs. The news from across the Bristol Channel was that the Grecians had kicked off 15 minutes late due to 'crowd congestion'. This meant that Exeter would play out the final stages of their game knowing exactly what they needed to do. Had this been deliberately engineered? Or was this payback for our own stolen advantage in another fixture against Hull four years before?

The news from Exeter was doubly frustrating for, while the game remained scoreless, Southend had missed a penalty. Just as it seemed fortune was smiling on Devon, luck showed an even hand. A rather fortunate handball decision went the Swans' way, Thomas slammed home his second penalty of the afternoon, and the Swans went into half-time level. Psychologically this was a massive boost, but the implications for the final 45 minutes were crystal clear. If the scores remained the same, the Swans were safe, but if Exeter grabbed a winner it would be too horrible to think about. A win was essential if we were not to have to suffer a quarter of an hour of excruciating agony.

The Swans came out with fire in their bellies after the break. Whether Brian Flynn had said something, or whether the penalty decision had restored belief that this was to be their day, the team came out fighting. Lenny Johnrose grabbed the lead after a goalmouth scramble – now the Swans' future was in their own hands. Hull looked beaten, but a one goal lead was never going to be adequate. When James Thomas completed his hat-trick with an audacious chip, the Swans were as home and dry as anybody could be on such a wet West Wales afternoon. As the final whistle went the crowd came onto the pitch and the celebrations began.

Meanwhile, Exeter played out their final minutes in the knowledge that they were relegated, and even their late winner was academic. Mike Lewis spent his Warholian 15 minutes of fame staring the Conference in the face. Later on he was to have rather more to think about, as the police investigated the running of Exeter's affairs. For many at Swansea, this added a sense of moral vindication to the relief of escape.

This had been a season of the highest drama, a roller coaster that kept everybody on the edge of their seats to the last. Survival by the thinnest of margins could not disguise how close the club had come to disaster. The words 'never again' were echoed throughout the club at every level. The lows of the season were too many to list, but three crucial home defeats by fellow strugglers Carlisle, Bristol Rovers and Exeter - when even draws would have spared the final drama - would have ranked high amongst them. Then again, it was not the Swansea way to do things the easy way.

Yet there were also many positives, even on the field of play. After years of prosaic football, there was now genuine hope that we had found a nucleus of players who could take the club forward, and play in a style appropriate to its self-image. The ball control of Leon Britton had at times been mesmerising, and his return to form and fitness in the final two fixtures was surely crucial. James Thomas had scored vital goals despite a barren spell when he was played out of position. Roberto Martinez appeared to be the midfield general we had sought for years.

Perhaps most important of all, the club now seemed to have some genuine momentum, a feel-good factor, and if the results of the last 20 games could be replicated over the entire length of the following season, a play-off spot was not out of the question. Even on a wet West Wales Saturday evening, the skies seemed to be clearing, and the future looked brighter than for many a year.

*   *   *

If James Thomas had grabbed the headlines on that epic final day with his hat-trick, most fans ascribed the club's survival to another player who had arrived that season. The upturn in form had coincided with the signing of Spanish playmaker Roberto Martinez, who had brought poise and guile for too long lacking in midfield. Suddenly, the Swans had a player who could impose his personality on a game, and around whom it seemed a team could be built. Martinez's route to South Wales had been somewhat unusual, as there were not too many Spaniards plying their trade in British football generally, let alone the lower divisions. He was the survivor of the so-called 'Three Amigos' signed by Wigan owner Dave Whelan from Real Zaragosa in 1997, arriving at the Vetch via Walsall. He had also shown himself to be an intelligent analyst on Sky Television's coverage of Spanish football, where he frequently encountered one John Benjamin Toshack. Indeed, Martinez cited Toshack as the reason he had become interested in the Swansea cause.

However, Martinez was hardly the first foreign player to appear for the club. As early as the 1960s, a Hungarian by the name of John Haasz had turned out for the Swans, while Dutch goalkeeper Nico Schroeder featured briefly in the mid-1970s. More famously, Toshack's team featured the Yugoslavs Dzemal Hadziabdic and Ante Rajkovic, although it rarely received the acknowledgement that was due for the espousal of a genuine European sweeper system based around the two imports.

The shrinking world of the 1990s saw an increase in the numbers of foreign players attracted to the British game by a combination of a developing global market, the Bosman ruling and the explosion of wage levels. While the earliest imports tended to be somewhat anonymous Scandinavians or world stars past their prime, the passage of time saw a broader spread of foreign talent arrive. There is little doubt that the best of these players brought a huge amount to the English leagues in terms of professionalism, skill levels and tactical awareness. Players such as Gianfranco Zola and Dennis Bergkamp were rumoured to remain behind at training to rehearse their skills long after their British counterparts had departed for the day. As wages escalated, so did the numbers of foreign players, and while there were the odd poor purchases, the vast majority raised standards in the British game immeasurably.

The foreign influx had knock on effects down the divisions, partly due to the displacement of some lesser lights from the Premiership, but also due to direct imports. A foreign player often cost less in terms of both fee and wages than a British counterpart, while their skill levels and professional habits were frequently superior. On the darker side, some players were hawked by unscrupulous agents, and signed by managers on the flimsiest of evidence. Rumours circulated regarding players supposedly signed on the basis of unsolicited videos, while questions were asked as to whether managers were receiving kick-backs. Former Arsenal manager George Graham was found guilty of this particular ruse, and some fans suspected that his activities were the tip of the iceberg.

Swansea City was no exception to the trend and fielded a number of foreign players in the period covered by this book with mixed success. Inevitably, perhaps, it was a foreign player-manager who began the process, although it was difficult to think of Jan Molby as being an overseas star. With his Liverpool accent and long career at Anfield, it was easier to think of Danny Kaye as being Danish. However, Molby had been developed, both in his homeland and subsequently at Ajax, into an exponent of the passing football that was associated with Denmark, Holland and Liverpool, and remained true to those principles during his time in charge at the Vetch.

It was therefore of little surprise when Molby brought in Portuguese defender Joao Moreira. The excitement amongst supporters about signing a player from a world famous club such as Benfica was tempered when it was discovered that the club of Eusebio ran a rather large number of teams. A tall fullback who frequently flattered to deceive, Moreira played in the Wembley play-off final, but was never guaranteed a place in the starting line up. Yet he was nowhere near as big a flop as Molby's compatriot Thomas Willer, a central defender who featured toward the end of the 1996-97 season. Some fans believed that the Dane's agent must have revealed similar imaginative skills to Hans Christian Andersen when describing his client's abilities.

The foreign influence grew to a peak in John Hollins' reign, during which time the Vetch Field dressing room came to feature a wide range of nationalities. Walter Boyd arrived in a fanfare of publicity in 1999, and made an immediate impact with two goals on his debut. Sadly, he could not maintain that momentum, and never looked likely to net 20 goals in a season, let alone achieve his stated aim of scoring 35 to break the club scoring record. Almost certainly Boyd would have benefited from having the ball played to feet, as his aerial ability was non-existent. Some fans questioned his attitude with racist overtones, implying that the Jamaican wasn't up for the cold wet nights of the English Third Division. It seemed more likely that Boyd's inconsistent form and sometimes negative body language were caused by a totally alien style of play.

Indeed, issues of suitability for the English lower divisions surrounded a number of overseas players signed by Hollins. Giovanni Savarese scored regularly upon first joining the club, but the goals dried up following his return from a head injury. Frenchmen David Romo, Matthias Verchave and Nicolas Fabiano all looked skilled, but did not acclimatise to the hurly burly of the Second and Third Divisions. Similar comments could be made of Nicolas Messina, who having escaped one economic disaster in his native Argentina, found himself at the centre of another as Tony Petty attempted to single-handedly re-write British employment law.

Arguably the most successful of Hollins' overseas imports was Mamade Sidibe. The Malian was reminiscent of Tore Andre Flo, with deft skills on the ground for a tall man. Certainly he added pace, skill and aerial ability to an attack that was too often predictable, and his partnership with Stuart Roberts looked promising. Unfortunately, frequent injuries restricted his appearances, and eventually led to him falling out with the club. Sidibe was quickly coveted by clubs in higher divisions, and one can hardly blame him for eyeing opportunities elsewhere. The Petty episode was surely disconcerting for any young player attempting to earn a living on foreign soil, and must have left him wondering what he had got himself into.

However, the majority of the overseas players signed by the Swans failed to make the desired impact, and left questions hanging as to their suitability. If the top level of the English league system had developed an overly physical style by the early 1990s, the lower divisions saw the trend exaggerated. Whether one blames coaches or over-permissive refereeing, the game at this level had too often degenerated into a grotesque parody of the game as played by the rest of the world.

While a few clubs, including the Swans under Burrows and Molby, attempted to keep alive the light, the beautiful game had in too many cases become distorted into a battle of brawn. Matters gradually improved at the top of the Premiership, partly due to the influx of good quality foreign players and coaches, and by the turn of the millennium some of the better British sides were successfully combining good technique with what had become the British norms of pace and physicality. However, further down the ladder the trend continued of clubs employing managers and coaches whose philosophy appeared chiefly influenced by Corporal Jones from television's *Dad's Army*. It seemed some clubs' coaching manuals didn't extend beyond the mantra, 'They don't like it up 'em!'

While the likes of Sidibe and Martinez appeared able to cross the cultural divide, many foreign players became lost in the maelstrom. Whilst it could be argued that the adaptability of those two players was evidence of a greater natural ability, there was an alternative view. Had British football in the lower leagues lost all connection with the game played in the wider world? Too many teams in Britain appeared to have abandoned the finer points of the game as a concept, and replaced them with physicality and, in extreme cases, intimidation.

Logically, one might have expected that the displacement of many British players from the Premiership might have seen the lower divisions develop a more skilful approach, but in practice this does not seem to have happened, while there is much evidence to suggest that the gap between the Premiership and the newly re-christened Championship has grown. If the Premiership is slowly aspiring to a more European style that combines the elements of the British and continental game, then should clubs lower down the league ladder not also look to improve on technical ability? Might not the extra edge so frequently sought by managers come through perfecting the slick passing frequently seen at all levels of many European countries rather than merely seeking new levels of physical advantage? Breaking the cycle will not be easy, and referees will surely have a part to play, but entertainment can surely only improve if inspiration is allowed to flourish at the expense of intimidation.

The reliance of the top British clubs on overseas players also raises issues regarding the development of young players, both in Britain generally, and at Swansea City in particular. There are legitimate concerns regarding the failure of the Swans to continue the tradition of producing good quality young players. Not only does it seem a waste if local talent is overlooked, but there is also the issue of identification between fans and the team.

There can be a tendency in some circles to hanker after the days when the composition of the side was primarily local. While some of the more extreme versions of this sentiment verge on xenophobia, there is a respectable argument that there is a stronger feeling of identification between fans and the team if at least some of the players are perceived as having their roots in the area. However, on any sensible basis, the composition of the team should always be determined by ability rather than birthplace. Fielding 11 locally born players is not the way forward unless those players are of truly good quality. Few fans would prefer a second-rate local combination as compared to a truly good team with a more cosmopolitan background. A good balance between local talent and recruits from the wider world is surely the ideal, as exemplified by John Toshack's side of the early 1980s.

Yet might salvation lie by looking at what is happening in foreign countries where there are ready supplies of talented young players? Might the Swans be helped in reversing the trend of diminishing numbers of players coming through the youth system by looking at our European neighbours? In particular it may be worth the club studying the approach taken by countries such as Holland and France who have been prolific in developing young players in recent times. Such a step may help address the technical gap that has grown between British football and that of mainland Europe. How could this be accomplished in practical terms?

The Swans have visited the Netherlands for pre-season tours in recent years. Might there be possibilities through their Dutch associates to develop a scheme whereby Swans' trainees receive coaching in Holland? In a world where businesses and educational establishments compete for the best recruits by offering opportunities in Europe, the club's traineeships might appear more attractive if they featured a period of Dutch coaching. As connections with mainland Europe become stronger in every walk of life, it makes sense for Swansea City to take advantage of the new opportunities and explore the possibilities with an open mind. Since the club's 'rebirth' in early 2002, it has moved toward a more European model in terms of ownership structure and stadium tenure. Might the club look to learn other things from Europe, in particular on the field?

*   *   *

If the 2002-03 season had been traumatic on the field, it ironically produced genuine reasons for optimism off it. Certainly the new board's honeymoon period had been short-lived, and they had been forced to mature very quickly. The board came through, if not exactly with colours flying, then certainly with credibility intact and valuable lessons learnt.

The previous season's sacking of Colin Addison had been controversial, and critics who believed that an experienced head was needed were vindicated in the early weeks of the season. Yet the board acknowledged their mistake, acted bravely, and came good when acceding to Brian Flynn's requests to upgrade the playing staff. Whilst it was difficult to know whether greater resources were made available to Flynn than to Cusack due to the club's parlous position, the new manager was undoubtedly able to use his contacts to bring in players who were of better quality.

More importantly, there were signs that Swansea and South West Wales rediscovered its football team. Attendances in the second half of the season seldom fell below the 6,000 mark, with two bumper gates in the final two home games. Possibly the threat of relegation from the

Football League galvanised many who for too long had taken the presence of professional football in the city for granted. The area has lost much in recent years and the recent absence of regular county cricket at St Helen's and the problems and changes at the rugby club emphasised that years of sporting tradition are no guarantee of future existence. In addition, there seemed to be a new mood abroad in the city recognising that, after years of frustration and suspicion regarding the true motives of those who ran the club, the current board had genuine football interests at heart.

Indeed, the Council seemed to reflect that change of perception, quickly agreeing a deal to ensure that a new stadium at Morfa would finally become reality. That after years of plans and prevarication, the stadium was now to actually be built spoke volumes as to how the Council perceived the new board as compared to their predecessors. Now the dream was to be realised, and for the 2005-06 season, Swansea City would have a new state of the art home.

The board had played their part in boosting gates through a concerted series of special offers on admission prices. Under previous regimes such attempts had smacked of tokenism, but this time around one sensed that the board were genuinely interested in reaching out to the potential fan-base and bringing back the missing thousands. Despite the struggles on the pitch, there seemed to be a genuine feel-good factor surrounding the club, and that sustainable growth was possible from a solid base. Meanwhile, the Trust built on the success of the anti-Petty campaign through contributing to the wages of Alan Tate and Marc Richards, and proved that it could make a continuing positive contribution to the well-being of the club.

Out of adversity, it seemed, was coming genuine strength. Not based on the extravagant promises of the loud-mouthed entrepreneur who might brandish his wallet but withdraw if a better opportunity came along. Not the flawed projections of a corporation which sought quick profits for its shareholders, but hold little in the way of long term commitment to the football club. This was the genuine strength of a community getting behind its heritage. The strength of ties that bind, not a marriage of convenience. Might Swansea follow the example of Charlton and Brighton where near brushes with death had resulted in rebirth as a stronger club, led actively by the people without whom it couldn't exist – the fans?

Season 2002-03 will go down as the season that Swansea City so nearly lost part of its tradition, its Football League status. This followed a season where the club could so easily have been lost for financial reasons. Yet ironically, for all the traumas, there was a feeling abroad that the club might just be in its best position for years, and that it could increasingly face the future with a degree of confidence.

Alan Tate (Photo: Andrew Thomas)

Lee Trundle without his famous haircut
(Photo: Andrew Thomas)

14. The boys of summer

The old cliché has it that football is a game of two halves. Prior to the World Cup in the United States in 1994 it was suggested that it become a game of four quarters. While this madcap idea never got off the ground, Swansea City conducted their own live experiment with division by four during the 2003-04 season. If the quarters were not even, there were four recognisable phases to the campaign, passing from ecstatic hope to consolidation, through distraction to disappointment. If some supporters were ultimately content with an unspectacular finishing position that avoided the trauma and excitement of the year before, this was still a far from straightforward season. It seems 'uneventful' is an adjective that has gone missing from the Vetch Field dictionary.

As the heat of the summer of 2003 baked South Wales, a positive vibration filled the air around the Vetch Field. If this was rather strange bearing in mind the club's brush with disaster just a few weeks earlier, the upturn in form and style of football in the second half of the season provided grounds for cautious optimism. The increased gates since the New Year were reflected in the best sales of season tickets since the close season of 2000.

Off the field, Huw Jenkins was named as chairman, with Supporters Trust representative Leigh Dineen as vice-chairman. There had been some criticism of a perceived lack of leadership during the 'committee' phase of the previous season, and this move filled the vacuum. It was also announced that in recognition of their efforts that the Trust were to have a second seat on the board. Meanwhile the board acted swiftly to end managerial uncertainty by offering Brian Flynn and Kevin Reeves new two year contracts, while Alan Curtis moved back to a role in youth development.

Flynn was obliged to get to work immediately, as almost the entire first team squad were out of contract, and a quick decision was needed on whom to retain. There were some predictable departures, as the long associations with the club of both Steve Watkin and John Williams were ended. Watkin had proved a good acquisition over the years, but sadly his crucial role in Hollins' team had been forgotten in a season where goals had been hard to come by, and all confidence appeared to have been lost as he became the butt of the crowd's frustrations. Williams had never truly recovered the form that had made him successful in his earlier spells at the club.

In fact, the departure list was not as long as it might have been, as most of Nick Cusack's signings had been unloaded during the course of the previous campaign. Matt Murphy was offered a new contract, but decided to retire. More contentious was the decision to grant Andrew Mumford a free transfer, although rumours about the previous season's Player of the Year suggested an attitude problem. Certainly Mumford's recent performances had failed to live up to his undoubted potential. More unlucky was Gareth Phillips (no relation to the author), whom few would criticise in terms of effort, while Terry Evans was deserving of sympathy. The whole-hearted full back's attempts to establish himself in the Football League had been hampered by serious injuries as a result of illegal challenges that finished each of his two seasons in February. When added to the injuries sustained by previous incumbent Steve Jones, it seemed that the Swans' right back position was something of a poisoned chalice.

New contracts were soon agreed with the nucleus of the squad who had successfully turned things around at the close of the previous season. Brad Maylett who had come in on loan from Burnley in the final weeks completed a full time move, as did full back Leon Hylton from Aston Villa. Andy Robinson, a former Tranmere reserve who had been playing in local league football in Liverpool was offered a trial, and subsequently a contract. Fans were given a huge boost when Flynn pulled off two major coups. First Leon Britton returned from West Ham on a permanent deal. Next, Wrexham striker Lee Trundle renewed the link with his former boss by moving south. Irish under-21 goalkeeper Brian Murphy moved from Manchester City in the hope of dislodging Roger Freestone, while Keiron Durkan and Karl Connelly who had also played for Flynn at Wrexham completed the squad.

On what seemed the hottest day of a burning summer, nearly 9,000 turned out to see the Swans defeat Bury 4-2 with Maylett scoring an unlikely hat-trick. A further three goal salvo from Trundle completed a comeback to win 4-3 at Cheltenham a week later and suddenly the team were flying, winning and scoring goals for fun. The football was arguably the best seen at the ground since the Toshack era. After ten games the team topped the Third Division, were leading scorers and Trundle topped the individual scoring chart for the division. The player nicknamed 'Magic Daps' had established himself as an iconic crowd favourite, a box of tricks topped off with a hairstyle reminiscent of Mr Whippy. Defensive frailty had been addressed by the return of Roger Freestone for the inexperienced Murphy, and the signing of former West Ham trainee Izzy Iriekpen.

Inevitably this was all too good to last, and the first quartile of the season drew to a close with an unfortunate 1-0 defeat in front of over 20,000 spectators in a top of the table clash at Hull's new stadium. If the opening phase had been characterised by the team winning in spectacular fashion, the second brought fans back down to earth. While results were good enough to stay in the play-off positions, the swagger of the early games had disappeared. Injuries to crucial performers such as Martinez, Maylett and Trundle certainly didn't help, but there may also have been a loss of the surprise element. The early season success had meant that teams now came to the Vetch to defend, and once the initial threat had been seen off, the Swans didn't seem to have an alternative strategy to break them down. Too often the pattern degenerated into a series of hopeful long balls aimed toward the head of Kevin Nugent.

162

Yet the side managed to grind out enough results by such pragmatic means to stay in the top six by Christmas, and with the return of injured players in the New Year, hopes remained high that a bid for promotion would materialise. Whilst Jason Smith had been forced to admit defeat in his long battle with injury and retire, the defence had been boosted by the return of Alan Tate on a further loan arrangement. When Yeovil were defeated 3-2 in a final thrilling match of the year at the Vetch through Trundle's last minute winner, it seemed the heady days of summer had returned. Sadly, flattery to deceive was to epitomise the season.

The third act of the drama in four parts was dominated by the club's best FA Cup performance since 1980. Yet there was a feeling that the highly publicised and lucrative cup run was diverting attention from a worrying loss of form in the league. It was to be the last week of February before the club won a league match in 2004. Included in this run were defeats at struggling Bury and Kidderminster, while a home loss to rivals Torquay highlighted the difference between the Swans and the genuine contenders at the top end of the Third Division.

Whether the cup had proved a distraction was debatable, many fans believing that the poor run was a disaster waiting to happen as certain basic personnel and tactical problems came to the fore. The signs had been there prior to Christmas, but disguised by the horrendous injury list. However, the explanation of lack of availability of key personnel no longer held water as these were now the same players who had dazzled in late summer. The one exception was Richard Duffy, who left to join Premiership Portsmouth for £175,000 after only a handful of first team appearances. As Duffy was available on a Bosman transfer at the end of the season, the club had little option, but the loss of one of the club's most promising young players highlighted the realities of lower division football in the new millennium. As some form of compensation, Alan Tate returned to the Vetch once more, this time making the move permanent.

Yet much was forgiven as the Lee Trundle show hit the FA Cup. Matters had started quietly with home victories over Rushden and Stevenage before Christmas. The Rushden victory had featured a spectacular goal by the much-maligned Keiron Durkan, leaving his numerous critics rubbing their eyes. If that was a contender for goal of the season, Trundle was not about to be upstaged, as he scored with a spectacular free kick against Macclesfield in the third round. Yet even that effort paled in comparison with Andy Robinson's set piece special against First Division Preston in the next round.

A packed Vetch had seen various surviving members of the 1964 team paraded before the match, but Preston had looked set to repeat the outcome of the famous semi-final as they led by the only goal with around 10 minutes remaining. In five never-to-be-forgotten minutes the game was turned on its head, and the Vetch erupted in inimitable style. First Robinson scored what most fans would consider to be the Swans best goal of the season, a 30-yard free kick hit with pace and precision that dipped into the top corner of the goal. The dead ball strike could not have been bettered by Beckham, Zola or Zidane. Within minutes Trundle added a winner that meant that he had scored in every round, and became a focus for national television, a welcome change from the 1999 cup run when the headlines were grabbed by Cyril the Swan.

When the draw pitted the Swans against Tranmere at Prenton Park there were high hopes of a first quarter-final since 1964. Although Birkenhead-born Robinson scored early to give Swans the lead, they were eventually themselves undone by a wonder goal to spoil the local boy's trip home. Yet while the money from the cup run was undoubtedly welcome, many felt the 2-1 defeat was a blessing in disguise. The decline in league form that had paralleled the cup run meant that the play-off spots were now 11 points away, and automatic promotion had long been regarded as fantasy. Optimistic souls hoped that a concentration of minds on the league could still secure a play-off spot, while pessimists thought of the fate of Shrewsbury, who 12 months earlier had seen a cup run blow up in their faces as they slipped down the league and finished in the relegation spots.

Thus a season that had started with such promise entered its final phase with hopes of a happy ending still flickering, but with serious doubts as to what could realistically be achieved. Stuart Roberts was brought back from his Petty-imposed exile at Wycombe to help boost supporters' spirits. Yet as with so much of the season, Stuart's return was to start brightly but fade away into ultimate disappointment. Back-to-back wins over Leyton Orient and Cambridge revived hope, while the football played in a thrilling 1-1 home draw with leaders Doncaster was considered the best since the turn of the year. Shortly afterwards, Paul Connor was signed for £35,000 from Rochdale, the first fee paid to another league club since the Cork era. Slowly, the horrors of the past few years were being laid to rest, and the club seemed to be showing they were back in serious business.

Unfortunately, however, the new signings did not revive the club's faltering league position and the dwindling hopes of a play-off spot were dealt a near-fatal blow by a defeat at struggling Macclesfield. Within days Brian Flynn and Kevin Reeves had departed, officially 'by mutual consent', with the pair's failure to move full-time to West Wales being cited.

The move divided fans between those who felt Flynn had revived the club by signing its most naturally gifted squad for years, and those who pointed to the serious decline in league form. Questions were raised over the squad's fitness levels, and rumours abounded regarding lax training schedules and poor off-field discipline. Flynn's tactical nous was once again called into question. There had been hints that the board were dissatisfied following the defeat at Bury in January, but to have sacked the manager in the midst of a lucrative cup run would have made little sense. Once the play-off hopes had been virtually extinguished, patience with Flynn had clearly run out. Alan Curtis took temporary charge, and the team responded with a fine performance in a 4-2 win over struggling Scunthorpe amidst a surreal stunned atmosphere. While romantics briefly dreamed of Curt leading an unlikely revival all the way to play-off glory, a 3-0 reverse at Huddersfield brought everybody down to earth and persuaded the board to act sooner rather than later.

While the local press produced a list of candidates that contained the *Casablanca*-like list of usual suspects, the club announced that the new manager was to be Kenny Jackett, a former Welsh international whose father originated from the Swansea area. Jackett had played all of his club football at Watford, where an early end to his playing career saw him build a future in coaching. His latest role had been assistant manager at a reviving QPR, and he arrived with a number of endorsements from his peers, and a fistful of coaching qualifications.

Jackett's reign got off to the worst possible start, with a 2-0 defeat at Rhyl in the FAW Trophy. Matters didn't improve in the league with five consecutive defeats at the hands of teams who still had much to play for, while the continuing injury problems didn't help. More pertinently, the team appeared to be physically hustled out of too many matches. This was a problem that first surfaced during the champagne football of early season, and while the romantic view was that the team should play their way to promotion, the reality of the Third Division was that on a week-by-week basis, physicality ultimately tended to win out. Jackett appeared to recognise the problem, moving Kris O'Leary forward from his normal defensive position, and securing his first Swansea win with a 2-1 success at Darlington.

While failure to secure a play-off spot and a final position of 10th was disappointing following the electric start to the season, the truth was that the club had already surpassed the previous season's points total with 12 matches to play. Throw in the cup run, and there was still a sense that the club had come a long way in a year. Perhaps the finale was an anti-climax following the nerve-jangling of a year before, but there had been more than a few positive highlights during the season. Certainly the crowds thought so, with an average gate in excess of 7,000.

With the club now emerging from the CVA, and the impressive skeleton of the new White Rock stadium rising fast on the banks of the Tawe, there was a sense that the club were moving forward. After years of broken promises, there was now to be delivery.

Compared to the position just over two years earlier, this was no small achievement. While there had been disquiet amongst certain sections of support over the sacking of Brian Flynn, the episode did show that the club were now not content to rest on their laurels. The final year of the club at the Vetch approached, and fans hoped for a celebratory farewell. Given Swansea City's record over the past dozen years, it was unlikely to be dull.

The main excitement of the second half of the season had come via the FA Cup although that competition had not been immune to change. Back in 1992 the FA Cup remained one of the major competitions in the British football calendar. Yet by the turn of the Millennium some people were questioning its relevance and very future. A national institution had eroded to become football's equivalent of the royal family – useful for helping tabloid newspaper sales, but considered of little consequence by those who now wielded genuine power.

Certainly it can be argued that the FA Cup is an anachronism, redolent of an age when Britain was more insular and deferential. The final was an occasion played at the Empire Stadium, frequently attended by royalty, where the crowd joined with a brass band to sing communal hymns. A Britain of steam-hauled "football specials" where the dapper Bryl-creamed stars of the England team travelled to provincial towns to be taught lessons in life by butchers and bakers in front of rattle-whirring crowds clad in scarves specially knitted for the occasion. This quaint *Pathé News* world seems light years away from its contemporary Sky Television version with its player cams and pro-zone.

Yet many of the traditions of the cup were in one sense anomalous by the time the seventies and eighties came around, without necessarily detracting from its fundamental appeal. The FA Cup final at Wembley remained a major annual event, regardless of whether by this time a considerable proportion of the crowd believed that far from being saved, the Queen ought to seek alternative employment. Indeed, the competing all day television orgies of the BBC and ITV reflected the huge interest in the final. The FA Cup's popularity had survived intact for over one hundred years, and maintained its appeal even when cultural changes meant that football itself faced an uncertain future. Why was it that when football was booming, the cup's future was being questioned?

Part of the problem lies with the riches generated by the expanded Champions League. Back in the early 1990s the FA Cup represented one of a limited number of roads to Europe. Moreover, the entrant to the European Cup Winners Cup might end up little worse off than the league champions if they made an early exit from the old style Champions Cup. Today even fourth place in the Premiership might let a club loose amongst the riches of the Champions League, with its extended fixture list. In comparison the FA Cup winners place in the down graded UEFA Cup competition seems small beer. The major clubs' priority now lies with a top four league finish than with winning the FA Cup. Similarly, for the mass of the Premiership, survival in the lucrative world of the top division is the primary aim of the season, particularly bearing in mind the potential financial consequences of relegation. The net result has been the frequent fielding of teams composed of squad members in cup-ties, particularly in the earlier rounds of the competition against lower division opponents.

Yet perversely, despite their somewhat equivocal attitude to the FA Cup, interest has also declined as the major clubs have come to dominate the competition. The chances of clubs such as Coventry, Sunderland or West Ham winning the competition have declined. The days of Manchester United falling at Bournemouth or Arsenal at Wrexham seem from a long gone era. It can be argued that the competition has lost its appeal not through the waning of the big club's interest, but because of their over-dominance, particularly when they seem to negotiate the 'banana skins' a little too easily. Has the Cup lost its greatest virtue, its unpredictability? Is it now perceived as merely reflecting the economic hierarchy of British football rather than its traditional role of challenging it? The FA Cup badly needed Millwall to give Manchester United something to think about in the 2004 final, rather in the way that Southampton and Brighton had done in the past. Instead the game degenerated into little more than an exercise in damage limitation, a brutal exposure of the gulf in ability between the two teams.

There are profound reasons for concern if the future of the FA Cup is under threat. The Cup has traditionally represented a link between the highest and lowest levels of the domestic game, and even in the modern age preserves some sense of unity, however superficial, that the league structure no longer can. It is questionable whether there will ever be another Swansea City sweeping up through the league system, let alone another Wimbledon going from the amateur ranks to the top of the professional tree. Even if for a day, the FA Cup gives the small team a chance to compete.

Yet it is difficult to see the FA Cup truly recovering its former status until more fundamental issues in British football are addressed. While the competition may be re-invigorated to some extent by the final's return to Wembley – however magnificent the Millennium Stadium may be, the competition and venue have become inextricably linked – it is difficult to see that the true romance can be recaptured as long as the major clubs can drift through the earlier rounds fielding weakened teams but dominate the later stages. Preserving the essence of the FA Cup seems dependant on dealing with the issues of competitiveness and income distribution in British football. The question marks currently against the future of the FA Cup are symptoms of a more pervading disease, and replicate those against the very soul of the modern game.

Traditionally, the British are said to love an underdog, and for all the noblest claims, *schadenfreude* is a major element in football. Most fans love to see the custard pies flying in the faces of the great and the good. The FA Cup was frequently football's equivalent of a Marx Brothers film where the anarchic and apparently hopeless prevail in the face of a bullying and arrogant establishment. This is the opportunity for the man in the Lada to get one over on the toff with the classic car collection. To that extent it can be said that the collective British psyche has changed little from the days when rattles were spun and hymns were sung at Wembley. There remains an inherent distaste for those who have become too big for their boots. The FA Cup must surely have a future if only for this trait of national character.

Certainly public disillusion was not the mood of most Swans' fans in the lead up to and aftermath of the cup runs of 1999 and 2004. The excitement of the draw hadn't diminished from that of 1995 or any earlier runs. The buzz around the city following the victory over West Ham was arguably the biggest since the Toshack era. If the win over Preston wasn't quite of the same order, it did set up the intriguing prospect of a run to the quarter-final or beyond. Even if the run of 2004 had never featured victories as legendary as those over Arsenal in 1926 or Liverpool in 1964, there is no doubt that had the team emulated their illustrious predecessors that they would have captured the imagination of Swansea and West Wales. Whether it can be defined as tribalism or as a more positive sense of community spirit, the FA Cup can enthuse and bring together an entire locality in a manner that other competitions fail to reach.

The chances are that Swansea City will never win the FA Cup, and the club's continued participation in a vibrant tournament is not a matter of self interest in that sense. In truth, the club's record over the years has led to as much humiliation as glory. For every Liverpool or West Ham there has been a Bognor Regis or Nuneaton to make Swans' fans cringe. Yet this is the do-or-die appeal of the competition, and without such an element of chance the romance will die. If the FA Cup is once again to recapture its place in the soul of Britain then the conditions must be made more conducive for the custard pies to fly. Sadly, in the opening years of the new Millennium that unpredictability seemed in the process of being lost. Many would say that football would be the poorer for it, yet until British football's financial and competitive equilibrium is re-calibrated it is difficult to be optimistic.

*   *   *

If the departure of Brian Flynn represented one major controversy of the 2003-04 season, a second was not long in coming. As the season drew to a close and the retained list was announced, it emerged that Roger Freestone was not to be offered a new contract. Swansea City would be starting the following August with a new number one between the posts.

In some ways it is appropriate that we leave the Swansea City story at the same time as Roger, for his career at the club coincides almost exactly with the period covered by this book. Joining during the 1991-92 season, Roger has been the one constant factor in all the teams discussed. From play-offs to cup finals, championship to relegations, through a series of management and ownership changes, the man from Newport has been the rock around whom the sands have shifted. From the relatively fresh-faced curly headed custodian of the early Burrows era, to the crop haired, gap-toothed veteran, one rarely had to enquire who would be standing in the Swansea goal. Young pretenders came and went, but Roger went on forever, or so it seemed. Indeed younger supporters probably don't recall anybody else being first choice in the green (or more recently multi-coloured) shirt.

Many fans were shocked at the decision, and almost everybody was sad to see Roger go. It has to be said that the end was not handled terribly well by the club from a public relations perspective. Some fans felt that the management could have had a word in Roger's ear as the season drew to a close, which would at least have given him a chance to bow out with a graceful retirement from the full-time game. Ironically, from reports on the press, it seemed that Roger had been enthused by Kenny Jackett's arrival, as he indicated that he believed that Brian Flynn was about to release him in any event.

While there was debate as to the handling of the affair, there was less surprise over the decision itself. Roger was 35, and while some goalkeepers have played on successfully to a higher age, time catches up with every player sooner or later. It may be better that Roger went out while still on top of his game. Recent years have seen the likes of Peter Shilton and Neville Southall play out their careers down the divisions with varying degrees of success, while David Seaman eschewed the guarantee of a farewell at the top in front of his adoring fans at Highbury for a half season at Manchester City that caused quiet muttering in the stands. All three might arguably have made more dignified exits if they had quit while ahead. The ageing process poses difficult questions of all of us in terms of assessing our own declining powers. Whether it is the nature of the position, which relies on reactions and judgement rather than speed and stamina, perhaps goalkeepers are not in as good a position to judge their decline as outfield players, and possibly only others notice the subtle changes that time and age bring. Whilst a few exceptional individuals have defied the ravages of time, perhaps the theory that all goalkeepers can play into their forties is a tad optimistic.

At least Roger had the satisfaction of finishing his career in an appropriate style, keeping a clean sheet in his final appearance, while fans who were at Darlington for his final away appearance will recall a typical reaction save to help preserve three points. The highlights of Roger's Swansea career were numerous. The penalty save in the Wembley shoot-out to clinch the Autoglass Trophy; the incredible acrobatic leap to palm away Neil Ruddock's potential equaliser in the FA Cup victory over West Ham; the record number of clean sheets in the Championship season; the fine performance to frustrate Brazil for so long in his only international appearance; the saves against Preston that helped a further giant-killing. More unusually there was the galloping goalie who ran the entire length of Oxford's Manor Ground to confidently slam a penalty past his opposite number, and join the ranks of goalkeepers with a league goal to their name.

Perhaps the most frustrating aspect of his departure for Roger was that he was so close to breaking the club appearance record. Just 21 games short, he would surely have beaten that record but for the injuries that kept him out for spells in both the 1998-99 and 2002-03 seasons. Sentiment suggested that it would have been appropriate for Roger to have played a further season, broken the record, and retired alongside the Vetch. Yet that same sentiment may have proved a fickle friend. As it was, Roger chose to retire from the full-time game and go back to his alma mater, Newport County, on a part time basis. In the event, further injury meant that this was to be a short-lived return.

Roger Freestone became synonymous with Swansea City for some 13 years. He ranks with the club's most famous and celebrated post-war goalkeepers, and has played a huge part in the club's recent history. His part on the field is well documented, but it should also be remembered that off it he played a role in helping to stop things falling apart in the dark days of the Petty nightmare. Whatever happened in the final season at the Vetch Field, it would seem odd not to see Roger taking his accustomed place between the Swansea posts. Another little piece of the club's history had passed on.

Andy Robinson (Photo: Andrew Thomas)

The North Bank at The Vetch, August 2002
(Photo: Andrew Thomas)

The club's new home: The Morfa Stadium rises on the bank of the Tawe
(Photo: Gary Martin)

15. Where do we go from here?

What then, can the future realistically hold for Swansea City? Can the club finally confound the doubters and re-establish itself in the upper divisions of what was once known as the Football League? Can it build a solid infrastructure and ensure that the mistakes of the past – be they under-achievement or overstretching – are not repeated? Will the opportunity be taken to finally fulfil its potential as one of the major sporting institutions of South Wales? Certainly the Swans stand on the cusp of a great historic opportunity with the move to the new stadium due to take place in the summer of 2005. In the meantime the club has emerged from the Company Voluntary Arrangement, and finds that it may be in a relatively strong financial position.

In the short term, the signs on the field are promising, as the club finished 2004 firmly established in the automatic promotion spots from the division formerly known as the third (or before that, the fourth). After a difficult opening few months in charge, and an inauspicious start to the 2004-05 season, Kenny Jackett appeared to have addressed many of the more obvious deficiencies in the team. The defence has been strengthened and given a major injection of physique in the shape of new signings Kevin Austin, Gary Monk, Sam Ricketts and Andy Gurney, while French goalkeeper Willy Gueret has successfully replaced the legendary Roger Freestone.

The side is less susceptible to being physically hustled out of games than a year earlier, and in this regard the deployment of either Kris O'Leary or Alan Tate in midfield has been influential. Although a little goal-shy during the opening months of the season, the team has gained a consistency and obduracy that is in many respects reminiscent of John Hollins' championship team of 1999-2000. While football can have the nasty habit of making even the most apparently cast iron predictions look stupid with hindsight, there does seem to be the genuine possibility that Kenny Jackett's squad could secure promotion before the stadium move.

Yet whatever the outcome on the pitch, there is a discernible feeling that the club is continuing to make progress following the traumas of the early years of the new millennium. For the first time in a long time there is a sense that it is building on strong foundations that could be the basis of sustainable growth. This has not been achieved by making wild promises, but rather through showing sensible levels of ambition. With finances stabilised and league status intact, there is the chance to build anew, and the club can do so at a time when the playing field in what has recently been re-branded as the Coca Cola League seems more even than for many a year. The days of too many clubs spending too much money on players of too little quality seem behind. Instead a new sense of reality has set in, and it appears increasingly that good players are available for sustainable wages. Conditions may be ripe for a well run club to succeed without breaking the bank, although those who over-extended themselves in the boom years may have a difficult journey ahead. Swansea City might just be in the right place at the right time.

How far this progress can take the club is, however, to some extent dependent on events outside the Swansea boardroom, and is dictated by happenings in the broader world of football. To repeat the observations made in the opening of this book, the football landscape in the winter of 2004-05 looks considerably different to that of the summer of 1992. While it seems that matters have to some extent levelled out between the so-called Championship and the newly re-christened Leagues One and Two, the huge financial gap between the Premiership and the leagues below suggests that it is highly unlikely that the club will be able to repeat the feats of the Toshack years in the near future. Statistics suggest that even if it was able to reach the Premiership its stay would be even briefer than on the last occasion the Swans played at the top level. Indeed, the experiences of the likes of Barnsley and Bradford following their stints in the Premiership would lead some supporters to question whether the Swans should again attempt to fly too close to the sun.

Certainly there might be a conflict of emotions for fans if the Swans were to ever again 'live the dream'. While it is natural for supporters to want to see their team take on the top names and play at famous stadia, there is nowadays the issue of the huge ticket prices demanded of away fans at many Premiership venues. How many Swans fans could afford to pay such prices on a regular basis? Moreover, it is also likely that if the Swans did manage to attain Premiership status the composition of the team would be very different from that of the Toshack era when the nucleus of the squad was home-grown.

Yet such concerns are hardly the exclusive preserve of Swansea City. Increasingly, questions are being asked around Britain as to the direction the game is being taken, and whilst one wouldn't hold one's breath on the basis of these problems being resolved in the short term, there are healthy signs that the supporter movement is leading a fight back. As the movement gains in momentum, there is hope that one day football's power-brokers will be forced to abandon their self-interested wilful deafness and act in the broader interests of the game as a whole.

To this extent Swansea City appear to be at the forefront of the new movement through the active participation of the Supporters Trust at the club. Much has been achieved in the last two to three years in terms of turning the club around and pushing it in a positive direction. However, neither board nor trust can afford to rest on their laurels. The achievements in saving the club, maintaining league status, completing the deal to move to the new ground and building a potentially successful team on the pitch are all laudable. However, thought must be given to the bigger picture of how the club can sustain growth. If the club were to stagnate in the near future, much that has been positive would be lost. The new set-up needs to ensure that it does not become merely a more democratic version of previous regimes.

It is sometimes easy in football to allow short term concerns to assume a disproportionate importance and lose sight of the bigger picture. Yet the board and trust need to work together to effectively re-build a club. To this end, they could do worse than to study the example of Charlton Athletic, particularly successful in re-inventing themselves as a well run community club. Indeed, Charlton provide the spiritual antidote to those who believe that promotion to the Premiership can prove a poisoned chalice to smaller clubs. By sensible management Charlton have bucked the trend, but have also in the process successfully expanded their community links.

Certainly, given the current financial realism running through football below Premiership level, there seems little reason why the Swans should not be able to compete at Championship (that's Division Two to older fans) level. For what they are worth, population figures from the 2001 census show that Swansea is a similar sized city to Southampton, only slightly smaller than Newcastle, Sunderland and Leicester, and considerably larger than either Portsmouth and Middlesbrough, let alone Ipswich or Norwich. Take in the surrounding hinterland and there is an ample constituency on which to build a fan base.

Moreover, the club also have a massive opportunity in that rugby union is not currently the huge counter-attraction it once was in South Wales. The shotgun marriage of the Neath-Swansea Ospreys is in its infancy, and in any event, the number of top fixtures in the new regional rugby schedule means that it is a limited counter-attraction. Whilst many fair-minded West Wales sports fans will take no comfort from the problems of rugby, there seems little doubt that there is an audience for live sport in the area whose attention is there to be won over.

The potential is surely there for the club to operate on a higher plane than has been the case through most of the last 40 years. However, if that potential is to be realised then the board must combine a realistic appraisal of the club's recent history with a well measured but pro-active approach. As we learnt from the Toshack years, great clubs are not built overnight. History teaches us that to spend large sums of money in over-optimistic anticipation of future income is a route to likely disaster. Further, if support is only skin-deep and based purely on short term results, it is likely to be fickle. Both on and off the field, growth needs to be sustainable in order that a gradually evolving team is playing to crowds who very definitely see themselves as Swansea City supporters.

To this extent the board and trust have work to do. While a winning team and the 'new stadium effect' will doubtless boost gates in the shorter term, those in charge need to ensure that local interest in the Swans is maximised, particularly amongst the young. Ticket prices should be pitched at a level that encourages attendance, and this is an area in which the trust can exert an influence as a lobbying force. To this extent the club will have to overcome the tendency of the local public to support the 'big event' but to be less keen to come out and support the team on a regular 'come rain or shine' basis.

Moreover, the club and trust should attempt to build links with various groups in the community with a view to convincing the uncommitted that Swansea City should be their club. Links with schools and other youth groups should be encouraged, and an active football in the community programme organised in association with the local council might also help address the problem of the apparent drying up of the well of talented footballers emerging from the area and playing for the club. It is a cliché, but youth is literally the club's future, both on and off the pitch. One *raison d'etre* of the trust was to preserve the club for future generations. There seems little point in doing so if those generations have either been priced out of the stadium, or have never had their interest stimulated.

The board and trust would also do well to bear in mind that if they are to build support that the ground must be a safe and pleasant place to visit. Problems of crowd behaviour including violence, racism and other unpleasantness need to be addressed, and action taken, where there have previously only been threats.

Whatever the future might hold, one thing is certain, and that the Vetch Field will no longer be part of the club's fabric. Whatever sponsor's name it eventually might bear, the stadium that started life known as the White Rock will provide an impressive new home for the club. The club will gain advantages through increased seating capacity, and the availability of modern corporate entertainment facilities, however much of an anathema these may be to the hard core fan. Experience at other new stadia around the country suggests that there may be a surge of interest on the back of the better facilities and sightlines, and the club should use the opportunity to persuade the ingénues to become regulars.

Moreover, one of the more unsung advantages will surely be that in moving to a municipally owned stadium the club will be spared the ongoing sole maintenance costs of a facility only used for income generation on thirty or so days per year. In other parts of Europe, a good quality municipal stadium is taken for granted. Perhaps it is appropriate that as the club has adopted an ownership structure not dissimilar to that often employed on the continent, that they should also move toward a more European model of ground tenure.

There's little doubt that leaving the Vetch after 93 years will be an emotive moment, and that many a tear will be shed when the final game takes place. There are so many memories, both personal and communal connected to the ground where the club has played throughout its existence. Many fans also fear that the vibrant atmosphere of the old ground will be lost forever, replaced by something bland. Yet there is also another way to look at things. For the majority of its history the Vetch has been host to disappointment and underachievement. Much as we may love it, might the Heath Robinson charm of the ground have contributed to this? Might the first class setting of future home fixtures prove more inspirational than the homely character of the Vetch?

Whatever the future at the new ground will hold, one thing is certain. From the moment the team sets foot on the pitch, new history and new legends will start to be made. The Vetch will never be forgotten by those who sailed in her, but once that first promotion is won, that first great cup victory registered, the first great goal scored, then we will soon settle into our new home. Football has entered a new era and the Swans are belatedly catching up. The Welsh national team has used its fixtures at the Millennium Stadium to help boost attendances to unprecedented levels. Can the Swans use the new stadium in the same way as an energising force?

The current resurgence of the club can ironically be traced to the forces unleashed by the hated Tony Petty, whose behaviour was so extreme that it helped mobilise the fans and dissipate the fatalism that had infected many supporters. Perversely, by becoming the fans' ogre, the former owner helped focus the energies of those who held the club close to their hearts. It can be argued that Swansea City is presently the property of it's supporters to a greater extent than at any previous time in its history. Over recent years the club has moved from being the personal property of a few people, through the great experiment with corporate capitalism to an ownership structure that represents a balance between private individuals and the mass of supporters. The board members are accepted as genuine Swansea City fans, while the ordinary fan can have some say in the development of the club via the trust. We no longer have to resign ourselves to be the passive consumers of a club that is our emotional property. This time around there is reason to believe that the new boss won't be the same as the old boss.

This is not to pretend that all will be plain sailing. Democracy throws up its own problems, and inevitably there will be those who will express disappointment over certain aspects of the way in that the club is being run. However, dissent has generally been in the minority thus far, and the majority of Swans fans appear to believe that the club is now being run sensibly by those with its genuine interests at heart. The presence of trust representatives on the board means that developments will be subject to scrutiny, and any future threats to the club's well-being can be brought into the public domain. That such matters are up for debate at all is evidence of how far both club and supporters have come since the eras of Doug Sharpe and Ninth Floor.

There is a temptation in this media age, as there has been since that first generation of children was exposed to television football, to seek glory and claim allegiance to one of the big teams of the day. However, when those teams win trophies then the glory will be a borrowed one, somebody else's victory shared for the price of a television licence or satellite subscription. When Swansea City win something, whenever and whatever that might be, it will be a victory that supporters can truly call their own.

Appendix: Summary of league results

Season	League	Pos	Pl	W	D	L	F	A	Pts
2003-04	Division 3	10th	46	15	14	17	58	61	59
2002-03	Division 3	21st	46	12	13	21	48	65	49
2001-02	Division 3	20th	46	13	12	21	53	77	51
2000-01	Division 2	23rd	46	8	13	25	47	73	37
1999-00	Division 3	1st	46	24	13	9	51	30	85
1998-99	Division 3	7th	46	19	14	13	56	48	71
1997-98	Division 3	20th	46	13	11	22	49	62	50
1996-97	Division 3	5th	46	21	8	17	62	58	71
1995-96	Division 2	22nd	46	11	14	21	43	79	47
1994-95	Division 2	10th	46	19	14	13	57	45	71
1993-94	Division 2	13th	46	16	12	18	56	58	60
1992-93	Division 2	5th	46	20	13	13	65	47	73